Black Americans of Achievement

Jesse Owens

CHAMPION ATHLETE

Black Americans of Achievement

LEGACY EDITION

Muhammad Ali

Frederick Douglass

W.E.B. Du Bois

Marcus Garvey

Alex Haley

Langston Hughes

Jesse Jackson

Coretta Scott King

Martin Luther King, Jr.

Malcolm X

Thurgood Marshall

Jesse Owens

Rosa Parks

Colin Powell

Sojourner Truth

Harriet Tubman

Nat Turner

Booker T. Washington

Jesse Owens

CHAMPION ATHLETE

Tony Gentry

With additional text written by
Heather Lehr Wagner

Consulting Editor, Revised Edition
Heather Lehr Wagner

Senior Consulting Editor, First Edition
Nathan Irvin Huggins
Director, W.E.B. Du Bois Institute
for Afro-American Research
Harvard University

CHELSEA HOUSE
PUBLISHERS
A Haights Cross Communications Company
Philadelphia

COVER: American athlete Jesse Owens relaxes at home.

CHELSEA HOUSE PUBLISHERS

VP, NEW PRODUCT DEVELOPMENT   Sally Cheney
DIRECTOR OF PRODUCTION   Kim Shinners
CREATIVE MANAGER   Takeshi Takahashi
MANUFACTURING MANAGER   Diann Grasse

Staff for JESSE OWENS

EXECUTIVE EDITOR   Lee Marcott
ASSISTANT EDITOR   Alexis Browsh
PRODUCTION EDITOR   Noelle Nardone
PHOTO EDITOR   Sarah Bloom
SERIES AND COVER DESIGNER   Keith Trego
LAYOUT   21st Century Publishing and Communications, Inc.

A Haights Cross Communications ⌁ Company

www.chelseahouse.com

First Printing

9 8 7 6 5 4 3 2 1

Library of Congress Cataloging-in-Publication Data

Gentry, Tony.
   Jesse Owens, champion athlete/Tony Gentry, with additional text by Heather Lehr
Wagner.—Legacy ed.
      p. cm.—(Black Americans of achievement)
Includes bibliographical references and index.
   ISBN 0-7910-8252-0 (hardcover) — ISBN 0-7910-8372-1 (pbk.)
   1. Owens, Jesse, 1913–   —Juvenile literature. 2. Track and field athletes—United States—
Biography—Juvenile literature. I. Wagner, Heather Lehr. II. Title. III. Series.
GV697.O9G463 2005
796.2'092—dc22

                                                          2004022052

Contents

Introduction

Nearly 20 years ago, Chelsea House Publishers began to publish the first volumes in the series called BLACK AMERICANS OF ACHIEVEMENT. This series eventually numbered over a hundred books and profiled outstanding African Americans from many walks of life. Today, if you ask school teachers and school librarians what comes to mind when you mention Chelsea House, many will say—"Black Americans of Achievement."

The mix of individuals whose lives we covered was eclectic, to say the least. Some were well known—Muhammad Ali and Dr. Martin Luther King, Jr, for example. But others, such as Harriet Tubman and Sojourner Truth, were lesser-known figures who were introduced to modern readers through these books. The individuals profiled were chosen for their actions, their deeds, and ultimately their influence on the lives of others and their impact on our nation as a whole. By sharing these stories of unique Americans, we hoped to illustrate how ordinary individuals can be transformed by extraordinary circumstances to become people of greatness. We also hoped that these special stories would encourage young-adult readers to make their own contribution to a better world. Judging from the many wonderful letters we have received about the BLACK AMERICANS OF ACHIEVEMENT biographies over the years from students, librarians, and teachers, they have certainly fulfilled the goal of inspiring others!

Now, some 20 years later, we are publishing 18 volumes of the original BLACK AMERICANS OF ACHIEVEMENT series in revised editions to bring the books into the twenty-first century and make them available to a new generation of young-adult readers. The selection was based on the importance of these figures to American life and the popularity of the original books with our readers. These revised editions have a new full-color design and, wherever possible, we have added color photographs. The books have new features, including quotes from the writings and speeches of leaders and interesting and unusual facts about their lives. The concluding section of each book gives new emphasis to the legacy of these men and women for the current generation of readers.

The lives of these African-American leaders are unique and remarkable. By transcending the barriers that racism placed in their paths, they are examples of the power and resiliency of the human spirit and are an inspiration to readers.

We present these wonderful books to our audience for their reading pleasure.

Lee M. Marcott

Chelsea House Publishers

August 2004

The Nazi Challenge

Adolf Hitler awoke on the rainy morning of August 1, 1936, looking forward to his grandest day yet as Germany's chancellor. He was to attend the opening ceremonies of the summer Olympics later that afternoon. The eleventh Games in modern history, the Olympic festival was slated to take place in his country's capital, Berlin, with 52 nations participating.

Three years earlier, shortly after he had come to power, Hitler said of the Games, "If Germany is to stand host to the entire world, her preparations must be complete and magnificent." To assure this, he had personally supervised a large part of the planning. With the help of 2,600 men, a stadium that could seat 100,000 spectators was erected out of stone on the western outskirts of the city. A swimming stadium, hockey arena, and dormitories for the athletes were also built. Century-old trees that bordered the city's avenues were dug up and moved to the athletic complex to make a park for the visitors.

Throughout the preparations, the Games were heavily promoted, often with colorful touches. The zeppelin *Hindenburg*, the world's largest airship, towed an Olympic flag across the Berlin sky. Thousands of people, from schoolchildren to soldiers, rehearsed for months, with marching bands and parading regiments slated to take part in the opening ceremonies. More than 3,000 runners were asked to carry the Olympic torch a kilometer each from Athens, Greece, to Berlin, so that the flame would arrive at the huge stadium just as the festivities were about to begin.

At precisely 3:00 P.M., a motorcade of sleek and powerful convertible limousines left Hitler's quarters, with the man dubbed the Führer (German for "leader") in the head car. The procession traveled down streets lined with flags bearing the Nazi swastika emblem before turning onto the rain-slick boulevard leading to the Olympic stadium. A fanatical shout went up from the thousands of people lining the route.

Dressed in his military uniform, Hitler stood in the front seat, his eyes set straight ahead. "The Leader came by slowly in a shining car," wrote American novelist Thomas Wolfe, "a little dark man with a comic-opera moustache, erect and standing, moveless and unsmiling, with his hand upraised, palm outward, not in Nazi-wise salute, but straight up, in a gesture of blessing such as the Buddha or Messiahs use." Following the limousines and motorcycles came a runner carrying the Olympic torch on the last kilometer of its 10-day journey.

The ovation that greeted Hitler's arrival in the main stadium was nearly matched by the cheers for the approach of the Olympic torch. As soon as the runner lit the huge fire bowl in the stadium, the procession of the athletes began. Hitler and the 100,000 other spectators stood to salute the representatives of all the nations that had come to compete. With martial music blaring over loudspeakers, the athletes marched smartly around the track. Among them were blacks, Jews, Hispanics,

German Nazi soldiers salute during the opening ceremonies of the XI Summer Olympic Games at the Lustgarten in Berlin, Germany. In the foreground is the Olympic torch.

Asians, and Arabs, none of whom fit the Nazi model of a proper human being.

The German coaches had purged their Olympic team of nearly every competitor who was not Aryan (Caucasian) and non-Jewish. Hitler would have preferred that the other nations do the same. Yet if they saw fit to enter what he considered "subhumans" alongside his Aryan athletes, then his team would simply have to defeat them, proving to the world the strength of his "racially pure" athletes.

Radio broadcasts and leaflets had blanketed Germany for months, promoting the brilliance of the nation's athletes, even as Jewish stars, born and raised in Germany, were hounded from the team. So the Games began, with Hitler's Aryans, cheered on by 100,000 spectators, facing off against everybody else. The cards, it seemed, were stacked. With the Germans on their home turf, the world was about to be taught a lesson.

THE WORLD'S FASTEST HUMAN

Competition began the next day, on Sunday, August 2. The first event was the preliminary eliminations of the men's 100-meter dash, generally considered the most glamorous of the track-and-field events because the winner has the right to call himself "the world's fastest human." German fans held high hopes for their best runner, Erich Borchmeyer, who Americans thought looked more like a football player than a runner. The Germans also had an eye out for the black American college student Jesse Owens, who held the world record in the 100-yard dash. As he stepped onto the rain-muddied track for his warm-ups, all eyes turned his way, wondering how the unassuming young man would do at this slightly longer distance.

Borchmeyer won his preliminary heat in a time of 10.7 seconds. An American sprinter, Frank Wykoff, bettered Borchmeyer's time by a hair in another heat.

Finally, just before noon, Owens got his chance. The hosts had furnished each sprinter with a silver hand shovel to help dig toe holes at the starting line (the aluminum-and-rubber starting blocks used by runners today were unheard-of then). Owens looked over the damp cinder track, which was already pocked and scarred by the feet of other runners, and got down on his knees to dig a foothold.

When the starter fired his gun, Owens shot off his mark, arms and legs pumping, even before the sound of the gun reached the upper seats of the stadium. In just a few steps he attained full speed. He ran with a fluid, easy stride; his eyes looked straight ahead, as if his only opponent were the tape stretched across the track fewer than 100 meters away. His feet hardly seemed to touch the ground.

Owens finished yards ahead of his closest competitor, coasting effortlessly across the finish line in a time that equaled the world record of 10.3 seconds. The crowd went wild. Even fervent Nazis could not ignore the speed of this young man.

That afternoon, Owens ran in the second round of heats. Again, he made it look easy. No other runner even came close during the race. This time Owens shaved a tenth of a second off his earlier standard, breaking the world mark. The judges decided that his time had been aided by the wind, however, so they could not award him the record.

That did not matter to Owens or to the crowd. He would run again the next day, and the next. Who could say how fast he might run in the 100-meter semifinals and finals? It was even possible that the 100-meter dash was not his best event. Didn't he also hold world records in the 220-yard dash and the long jump? Moreover, he was clearly at the top of his form, prepared to trounce all comers beneath the gray skies of Berlin.

German youngsters seeking autographs eagerly surrounded Owens on the way back to his room. On the very first day of the Olympic Games, he had proved a sensation. With speed

IN HIS OWN WORDS...

Hitler viewed the 1936 Olympics as an opportunity to showcase the new future he was carving out for Germany, but Jesse Owens ignored the competition's political focus that year:

I wanted no part of politics. And I wasn't in Berlin to compete against any one athlete. The purpose of the Olympics, anyway, was to do your best. As I'd learned long ago from [coach] Charles Riley, the only victory that counts is the one over yourself.

Jesse Owens waves from an open car during a ticker tape parade along New York City's Broadway Avenue. Owens was celebrating the four gold medals he won at the 1936 Summer Olympics in Berlin, when he was only 22 years old.

and grace he had proved that Hitler's Aryans were not superior to all others.

Jesse Owens upstaged Adolf Hitler at what was meant to be a triumphant display of German prowess. He performed as no one has since, captivating a worldwide audience and proving the falseness of the Nazis' racist notions.

Within the span of a week, Owens would become an international hero, prompting people everywhere to wonder who this incredible athlete was, where he had come from, and how he could possibly be so fast.

"Fighting the Wind"

James Cleveland Owens was born on September 12, 1913, in Oakville, Alabama—unimaginably far from the lights and fanfare of Berlin. Nicknamed J.C., he was the 10th (and last) child of Henry and Mary Emma Owens. He had six brothers— Prentice, Johnson, Henry, Ernest, Quincy, and Sylvester—and three sisters: Ida, Josephine, and Lillie.

Like thousands of families, black and white, throughout the South, the Owens family lived as sharecroppers. This meant that a local landowner, Albert Owens, allowed them to live in a ramshackle house on his property and use his farm equipment in exchange for their hard work and half the season's crop from the land they farmed. The Owens family sold the other half of the crop, and with the little bit of money they earned they bought clothing and a few basic supplies.

A predominantly white community of 1,000 residents, Oakville was situated along a red dirt road amid the rolling hills and tall pines of northern Alabama. Most of the Owenses' neighbors were sharecroppers, too. They plowed the fields in the spring with a mule, hoed the long rows of corn and cotton throughout the scorching summer, then picked cotton from sunup to sundown during the backbreaking two-week-long harvest in the fall. It was a constant struggle to make their harvest money stretch through the winter.

With so much work to be done, all the Owens children were expected to pitch in. The youngest son, J.C., was not able to work like his brothers and sisters. He was small and sickly, and he needed to be nursed through one cold winter after another, a hardship for a family that lacked the funds to pay for medicine or a doctor. As the drafty old house rattled with every icy blast, little J.C., wrapped in soft cotton feed sacks in front of the stove, coughed and sweated and cried with pneumonia for weeks at a time.

As if that were not enough, terrifying boils appeared on J.C.'s chest and legs. His father had to hold the crying child while his mother practiced makeshift surgery in her own home, carving the boils out of his flesh with a red-hot kitchen knife. Years later, in his autobiography, *Jesse*, Owens recounted one of those doctoring sessions in all its harrowing detail: "Real pain is when you don't have any choice any more whether to cry or not, and then maybe you don't even cry because it wouldn't help. I always hated to go to sleep at night, but now for the first time in my life I wanted to pass out. Something inside wouldn't let me. All I felt was the knife going deeper, around and around, trying to cut that thing loose, all I saw were the tears running down my father's face, all I heard was my own voice—but like it was somebody else's from far-off—moaning, 'Aww, Momma, no . . .'"

FIGHTING THE WIND

Through sheer will and the determination of his long-suffering parents, little J.C. somehow survived these brushes with death.

By the age of six, he was well enough to walk the nine miles to school with his brothers and sisters.

School amounted to a one-room shack that doubled on Sunday as the Baptist church for the blacks of the area. The teacher was anybody who had the time and the inclination. During spring planting and at harvest time, students worked the fields instead of arithmetic problems. In spite of all the drawbacks and interruptions, J.C. learned to read and write.

Meanwhile, his parents struggled to make a better life. First, they moved their family to a larger farm in Oakville, where they worked 50 acres of land, still barely able to make ends meet. The children endured the hard times by concentrating on happier moments: fishing, raccoon hunts, swimming, berry picking, games of hide-and-seek, and pranks. "We used to have a lot of fun," Owens recalled. "We never had any problems. We always ate. The fact that we didn't have steak? Who had steak?" His family, like most sharecroppers, did not think of themselves as poor because all their neighbors were poor, too.

With hard work and good weather, a family could pick enough berries for jams and collect enough wind-fallen apples, pears, and peaches to last through the winter. They canned tomatoes and beans from their garden and slaughtered a hog after harvest time. Even though the Owens family did not have much money, there was usually enough to eat.

Even with all that, there was time for play. It was in the low hills of Alabama that J.C. first began to run. He recalled in his autobiography that even as thin and sickly as he was, "I always loved running. I wasn't very good at it, but I loved it because it was something you could do all by yourself, and under your own power. You could go in any direction, fast or slow as you wanted, fighting the wind if you felt like it, seeking out new sights just on the strength of your feet and the courage of your lungs."

As the Owens family continued to eke out an existence from the red dirt of Oakville, prospects of better opportunities beckoned at last. One of J.C.'s sisters, Lillie, had moved to Cleveland, Ohio, and she soon wrote home that she had found work there earning more money than she had ever seen before. She begged her parents to pull up roots and join her in this worker's paradise.

Henry and Mary Emma Owens, however, did not jump at the chance to leave their tattered farmhouse amid the cotton fields. The Owens family had roots in northern Alabama that ran back for a century, into slavery days. They had never known anything but farm life. As fellow members of the Baptist church, their friends and family spread for miles around in the northern Alabama hills.

J.C.'s father understood particularly well how ill equipped he was to face urban life. He had never learned to read or write or even to calculate the value of the cotton he harvested. He was a good farmer and a well-respected deacon of the church, but none of that would matter in the big city.

J.C.'s mother argued strongly in favor of the move to Cleveland, countering each one of his father's reasons for staying in the south with an argument proving that Cleveland could only be better. When he reminded her how unschooled he was, she asked him if he wanted his 10 children to grow up just as ignorant. When he told her how he would miss the farm life, she waved her hand through their dark, unpainted rooms, showed him the all-but-empty kitchen shelves, ran a finger through the holes in her apron, and laughed.

For Mary Emma Owens, the family had nothing to lose and everything to gain from catching the first train north. When J.C. turned nine years old, they sent him down the road to sell their mule to a neighbor. With that money, they all bought train tickets, and as their youngest child later recalled, he stood with his folks on the platform at the Oakville station and asked, "Where's the train gonna take us, Momma?" She answered only, "It's gonna take us to a better life."

CLEVELAND'S EAST SIDE

That better life, however, lay a little more than a train ride away. The Owens family moved into the only apartment they could afford, in a ghetto neighborhood on Cleveland's East Side. Back in the country, the view beyond the windows of their house had expanded for miles across open fields beneath the limitless blue sky of Alabama. In the city, their windows opened onto bedraggled alleys and the walls of the building next door. Emma Owens more often than not kept her curtains closed.

Now that she had convinced the family to move north, J.C.'s mother was not about to forget her dream. She took jobs all over town, cleaning houses and washing laundry and put her daughters to work doing the same. The older sons took jobs in a steel mill, where the foremen appreciated the strength and endurance the Owens boys had developed in the fields. J.C., too young for such grueling labor, found a part-time job polishing shoes and sweeping up in a cobbler's shop.

For Henry Owens, who was in his 40s, the move north had perhaps come too late. Worn down by a lifetime on the farm, he could not keep up with his sons in the mill and had to settle for whatever part-time work he could find. Still, for the first time in his life, his labor earned him a paycheck. At the end of the week, the family pooled its money to buy luxuries they had only imagined in the South: new shoes, new clothes, and good, sturdy furniture.

The bustling city swirled about them. Mill work proved exhausting and closed in, run by time clocks and strict supervisors. Shysters waited on every corner to cheat a man out of his wages. Around the dinner table in their ghetto home, the Owens family acted out a story repeated in millions of urban households all over the country during the first half of the twentieth century—that of rural people in crowded apartments, bewildered and harried by their new environment, weighing in their minds the advantages and disadvantages of the move they had made to the city.

Jesse Owens and his family moved into the only apartment they could afford, in a ghetto neighborhood of Cleveland's East Side, shown here. Jesse had sold the family mule to pay for train tickets after his sister had implored her parents to move to a better life in the city.

And if the working life seemed worlds apart from the farm, 10-year-old J.C. discovered that Bolton Elementary School was just as far from the one-room schoolhouse back home in Oakville. Everything at Bolton ran in a businesslike fashion. For example, when the busy teacher asked for J.C.'s name, she misunderstood his slow Southern drawl and wrote it down as "Jesse." Afraid to interrupt her on his first day of school, the youngster took his seat without comment, and for the rest of his life he was called Jesse instead of J.C.

Unsure of how much schooling her new student had previously received, the teacher assigned Jesse to first grade, where he towered over his younger classmates. The little school in Oakville had taught him enough, though, so he quickly moved up to another class. Even so, he was a couple of years older and a few inches taller than the other children in his classroom.

Bolton, like the community it served, was a racially mixed school. Jesse soon made friends with children from all over the world—Poles, Hungarians, Greeks, Italians, and Chinese. He ran himself ragged exploring his new neighborhood, which seemed so much larger, more exciting, and more dangerous than the fields of Alabama. His imagination ran wild. In Cleveland, it seemed, all that limited anyone was how well their legs could keep up with their dreams. For children like Jesse—more energetic, more inquisitive, less set in their ways than their parents were—even a large city's ghetto could seem like a wonderland.

Jesse Owens spent the next three years of his life that way. In addition to working at the cobbler's shop, he held jobs in a greenhouse watering plants and as a grocery store delivery boy. The Northern winters, however, kept him in bed fighting pneumonia for weeks. When the time came for him to enter junior high school, Owens probably felt that he knew all about city life. No longer the awkward Southern hick, he stayed out of trouble, went to church on Sunday with his parents, and played a mean game of stickball.

At Fairmount Junior High School, Owens's life gradually began to diverge from that of his playground friends. All in one week he met the two people who would change his life. Each in his or her own way would show him a glimpse of a larger world than the one he knew on Cleveland's windy streets and then dare him to chase it.

The first person was a pretty young girl named Minnie Ruth Solomon. Minnie's parents had been sharecroppers in Georgia and had just recently moved north to try their hand in the city. As Owens recalled in adulthood, for the 14-year-old boy it was love at first sight: "She was unusual because even

Jesse Owens met Minnie Ruth Solomon at Fairmount Junior High School in Cleveland. He later recalled that even at age 14, he was in love: "I fell in love with her some the first time we talked, and a little bit more every time after that . . . ." Ruth and Jesse would later marry.

though I knew her family was as poor as ours, nothing she said or did seemed touched by that. Or by prejudice. Or by anything the world said or did. It was as if she had something inside her that somehow made all that not count. I fell in love with her some the first time we ever talked, and a little bit more every time after that until I thought I couldn't love her more than I did. And when I felt that way, I asked her to marry me . . . and she said she would." Jesse and Ruth were still too young for marriage, but their puppy love would grow.

The second important person Owens met at junior high was a short, skinny man with a whistle around his neck: Charles Riley, who coached the school's track team. Riley somehow saw potential in the happy-go-lucky kid from Alabama, even though he wasn't the strongest, fastest, or even the healthiest student in school. He called Owens into his office one day and asked if he would be interested in running a little after school.

3

"Four Years From Next Friday"

The teachers at Fairmount Junior High School knew that most of their students would never go on to high school. In the East Cleveland ghetto, bright youngsters had to grow up fast, helping their families earn a living any way they could. So classes skimmed over English, history, and mathematics, concentrating instead on the kinds of lessons that might help students find and hold jobs as laborers. Boys learned to use tools; girls were taught how to type and cook. Arriving on time, dressing cleanly, and following instructions meant more than test scores did.

Jesse Owens thrived under these conditions. Friendly, compliant, a fastidious dresser, he had never been a whiz at textbooks. Fairmount rewarded his strengths and did not penalize him for his weaknesses.

Meanwhile, a passion began to occupy Owens's imagination "so completely," he said, "that whole days would pass when I didn't think of anything else." He began to think of himself as a runner. Coach Charles Riley set up a training schedule for Owens, even though he was too young to compete on the school's track team. Because the youngster held part-time jobs after school, he asked the coach if it would be all right to train in the morning. Most days the two met at dawn, one sipping coffee and watching while the other stretched and jumped and ran.

It was not long before Owens began to look up to Riley almost as a second father. He even called the Irishman "Pop." The coach made sure Owens ate well, bringing him breakfast from his own table or inviting him to dinner with his family. He used their training sessions not only to build up the runner's legs and lungs but to build character as well. Riley told all of his teenage charges not to expect immediate results but always to train for "four years from next Friday." Steady, gradual improvement was the goal.

Riley may have been the first man Owens had ever met who challenged him to test his limitations. Having inherited from his mother the drive to achieve, Owens found in Riley a teacher who woke up early every day to hammer the point home that the biggest obstacle anyone has to overcome is within one's own head. Riley said that a man has to push himself every day, winning out over the tricks his mind plays on itself, in order to reach his potential. Yet he was not one to preach. He taught by quiet example and encouragement.

In the 1920s, most world-class sprinters tried to power down the track, furiously pumping their arms and legs. Riley thought this was unnatural. One day he took Owens to a racetrack to see the relaxed grace of the thoroughbreds as they ran, their hooves seeming to barely touch the turf, their eyes always looking forward, a study in speed. He told Owens and his other students to mimic the horses, to run as if the track were on fire, keeping each foot on the ground for as little time as possible. These characteristics became the hallmark of Owens's running style throughout his career and, through his example, revolutionized the way sprinters everywhere learned to run.

For a year, Coach Riley put Owens through his paces. Then one day he decided to time Owens at the distance of 100 yards. When Owens flew past the coach 11 seconds later, all Riley could do was stand there in openmouthed astonishment. He asked Owens to run the distance again, and again the runner clocked in at 11 seconds—unbelievably fast for a 15-year-old. It was time to suit this youngster up for the team.

Riley knew that with such speed Owens would make a good jumper. He signed Owens up to compete not only in the 100-yard and 220-yard dashes but also in the long jump and high jump. Sometimes, Riley entered him in the hurdles or the 440-yard run, guessing that these races would make the sprints seem easier. Owens quickly repaid his coach's confidence. In his first year on the track team, he broke the world record for junior high school students in the high jump and long jump. When Charlie Paddock, an Olympic gold medalist in the 100-meter dash, came to the school to deliver a speech, Riley introduced him to Owens. From the moment the two shook hands, Owens's only dream was to reach the Olympics.

A ONE-MAN TEAM

As Owens trained ever harder, life at home threatened to dash his dream. His father broke a leg when he was hit by a taxicab, and because of the injury he lost his job. Jesse's brothers, one after the other, were laid off from the steel mill, and when they could not pay their rent they moved their wives and children into their parents' already crowded house. These were the years of the Great Depression, when the nation's economy all but collapsed. Poor people, holding down the most tenuous of jobs, took the brunt of the hard times. Millions of workers all over the United States found themselves penniless and hungry, standing on food lines.

The pressure was great for 17-year-old Jesse to drop out of school and do what he could to help the family make ends meet. Credit must go to his mother, who, despite her tough days washing laundry for pennies, convinced her son to continue his education. In 1930, Owens enrolled at East Technical High School, a few blocks from his house. He tried out for the football and basketball teams but soon gave them up when they cut into his running time.

The track coach at East Tech, Edgar Weil, was not the inspiring innovator that Coach Riley had been. Luckily for Owens, Weil soon asked Riley to be his assistant, and under Riley's continued tutelage Owens came into his own. In the spring of 1932, during his junior year, he proved so dominant a competitor that one newspaper called him a "one-man team." That estimation was not far off the mark. Owens often scored more than half the points for his whole team at track meets.

Again private life intruded on Owens's ambitions. His girlfriend, Ruth, reported one day that she had become pregnant. The two hastily eloped to Pennsylvania in a car driven by a friend, David Albritton. The young couple claimed that they were married in Erie by a justice of the peace. It is more likely, however, that Owens and Solomon did not go through with the wedding, for no marriage license exists from that time. In any event, when the two lovers returned to Cleveland, they faced the wrath of their parents. Ruth's father swore never to let Owens see his daughter again.

Owens could do nothing but concentrate on his running. That summer, he took a big step toward realizing his dream, traveling to Northwestern University to try out for the U.S. Olympic team. Unfortunately, 1932 was not to be the year of Jesse Owens; he did not make the team. In both the 100-yard and 220-yard dashes, he lost to Marquette University sprinter Ralph Metcalfe, who went on to win silver and bronze medals at the 1932 Olympic Games in Los Angeles. Metcalfe was a powerhouse runner of the old school. He and Owens would

In 1933, Jesse Owens was a senior in high school and the star of East Technical High School's track team. This was the time of the Great Depression, and though the Owens family was struggling financially, Jesse's mother convinced him to finish his high school education.

become firm friends—and archrivals—in the years ahead. (For additional information about the 1932 Olympic Games, enter "Olympic Games 1932" into any search engine and browse the many sites listed.)

When the Olympics were over, some of the runners toured the United States, holding demonstration track meets. It must have come as some consolation to Owens that he won the 100-yard and 220-yard dashes and even finished second behind the 1932 Olympic gold medalist in the long jump, Edward Cordon, when the squad came through Cleveland. No matter how Owens felt about his performances, he gained valuable experience in competing on an international level.

Owens could not keep his mind entirely on his running, however. On August 8, 16-year-old Ruth gave birth to their baby. A healthy little girl, she was given the name Gloria Shirley. With this, Ruth's high school days were over. She dropped out of school and took a job in a beauty parlor. She continued to live with her parents, who still would not let Jesse in the house.

By refusing him the responsibilities of fatherhood, the Solomons, perhaps unwittingly, did Owens a favor. Now he could enter his senior year of high school and continue his track-and-field career. As a testament to his popularity, his East Tech classmates (95 percent of whom were white) voted him student body president. As the high scorer and natural leader of the track team, he became squad captain as well.

BREAKING RECORDS

Owens repaid his admirers with electrifying performances, not losing a race all year. Though he never deliberately drew attention to himself, he was so clearly head and shoulders above the other competitors that all eyes stayed on him, whether he was running a race or landing in the long-jump pit. On May 20, 1933, he concluded his high school career in typically splendid fashion. At the state interscholastic finals that day, he broke the world record for high school students in the long jump, sailing 24 feet, 3 1/6 inches.

Then, in June, at the National Interscholastic Meet in Chicago, Owens eclipsed even his own standards. In the 100-yard dash, he tied the world record of 9.4 seconds. In the long jump, he improved his best leap by a remarkable six inches. Then, in the 220-yard dash, he ran a blazing 20.7 seconds, breaking the world record.

Cleveland officials were quick to honor the city's new favorite son. They organized a victory parade as soon as Owens got home. Henry and Mary Emma Owens rode next to Jesse in the backseat of a convertible for the slow-moving procession along the broad streets downtown. In the car directly behind theirs rode Charles Riley.

When the procession stopped at City Hall, the mayor of Cleveland joined several council members in praising the young athlete, happy to discover a hero during such difficult times. They predicted a grand future at whatever college he chose to attend.

Owens let none of the fanfare go to his head. He drove a hard bargain in negotiating with the big midwestern schools that were clamoring for his talents. During the summer, Coach Riley drove Owens all the way to the University of Michigan to tour the campus. In the end, Owens elected to stay close to home. Ohio State University, in the state capital of Columbus, won the budding star.

In those days, colleges did not give athletic scholarships. Instead, they offered easy jobs at good wages to help students pay their way. After school each day, Owens would have to run a freight elevator at the State House. Having held much more strenuous jobs most of his life, he quickly agreed. Owens even secured a custodial job on campus for his father, but Henry Owens did not want to move again. He chose to stay home in Cleveland and appreciate his son's exploits from a distance.

There was one major hitch in all these arrangements. Owens had just slipped by with a D average in high school, and his report card failed to impress the administrators at Ohio State. The coaches got around this difficulty by having Owens take special tests over the summer. When he passed these, the last door opened.

With the next few years decided upon, Owens could tie up loose ends at home. For spending money, he pumped gas at a filling station. At long last, the Solomons gave in to their

Mayor Ray T. Miller of Cleveland (center) shakes Jesse Owens's (shown second from right) hand. It was 1933, and Owens had broken his own records at the National Interscholastic Meet in Chicago, Illinois. Cleveland officials organized a victory parade in Owens's honor.

daughter's pleas and allowed Owens to visit after work each day. On weekends, Riley drove him in his Model T to track meets. Once, they even drove as far as Toronto, Canada, for an international competition.

With autumn approaching, the old coach prepared to say farewell to his surrogate son. Pop Riley had started Owens out on the road to glory, instilling in him a will to win and humility toward the tasks that would face him in the years ahead. Owens was 19 years old, already arguably the world's fastest human. The rest would be up to him.

4

Countdown to the Olympics

Jesse Owens was among the handful of blacks that enrolled in an American university in 1933, when the Great Depression caused an unusually low percentage of high school graduates to enter college. Nevertheless, at Ohio State, a school where athletes—particularly football players—are treated like conquering heroes, he fit right in. The coaches made sure he signed up for easy courses, knowing that his secondary schooling had not been the best. The job running a freight elevator was even easier. Because freight was rarely delivered during his shift at night, he had hours of free time to study on the job. Finally, Owens learned that he could make extra cash traveling about the state on weekends, giving speeches to help promote the school. At that rate, he later recalled, he not only paid for his education but saved enough to send regular checks home to his mother and to help Ruth raise their baby.

Meanwhile, every day, Owens trained for the track season. In January 1934, without ever having run a race in college, he was named to the Amateur Athletic Union (AAU) All-American Track Team. Everything seemed to go well during the first semester, with the exception of his classwork. East Technical High School in Cleveland had done little to prepare Owens for a college curriculum, and having never learned how to study, he quickly fell behind his classmates. At the beginning of the spring semester, he was put on academic probation and ordered to bring up his grades.

Ohio State's track coach was a young man named Larry Snyder. A character builder as well as a coach, Synder was a younger, peppier, more ambitious version of Pop Riley. Snyder liked the natural running style Owens had developed in high school, but he believed there was still room for improvement. In the sprints, he concentrated on getting Owens to relax even more—he tended to tense his upper body and arms—and he taught the freshman a more compact crouch at the starting line, which would help him uncoil quickly into a full-speed run. In the long jump, Snyder showed the freshman how to "run through" the air, pumping his arms and legs for more distance as he flew. A dedicated student when it came to track and field, Owens practiced these new techniques with a diligence he rarely applied to his schoolbooks.

According to collegiate rules, Owens, like all incoming students, was not eligible to compete on a varsity team until his sophomore year. After another summer spent pumping gas back home in Cleveland, he traded in his job running the elevator for a more prestigious position as a page for state legislators in the capitol. When he joined the varsity track squad later in the year, the refinements Coach Snyder had taught him began immediately to pay dividends. On February 9, 1935, in his first Big Ten Conference meet, Owens won 3 out of 4 events, placing second in the 70-yard low hurdles.

Owens at a training session with his track coach at Ohio State University, Larry Snyder. "He was constantly on me," Owens said, "about the job that I was to do and the responsibility that I had upon the campus. And how I must be able to carry myself because people were looking."

It was plain to all concerned that he would be able to compete successfully on the college level.

TRACK AND FIELD SUPERSTAR

For seven intense years, Jesse Owens had trained to run and jump with the best, and at the Big Ten Championships in Ann Arbor, Michigan, on May 25, 1935, that training paid off. In the space of 45 minutes, Jesse Owens broke 5 world records and tied another. This feat has never been equaled; it is still considered the greatest single performance in the history of track and field.

Owens's teammates could not believe their eyes. They had seen him wearing hot packs on his back all week after falling down a flight of steps at school. When Coach Snyder, wary of aggravating the injury, wanted to bench him for the meet, they had overheard Owens pleading for the chance to run. Owens later said that he knew he would be all right when he first crouched down for the 100-yard dash. Miraculously, the pain seemed to disappear. After the starter's pistol sounded, Owens did the same, blazing effortlessly into the lead and tying the world record of 9.4 seconds.

In the 220-yard dash, Owens shaved four-tenths of a second off his previous best time, reclaiming the world record. He was also awarded the international record for the slightly shorter distance of 200 meters without having to run that race. Then, in his worst event, the 220-yard low hurdles, he breezed to a new standard of 22.6 seconds. In this race, he finished 10 yards ahead of his nearest competitor. Again, he was allowed the low-hurdles record for the shorter international distance of 200 meters.

It took just one leap for Owens to break the world record in the long jump. At his request, a friend placed a handkerchief beside the pit at the 26-foot mark. Owens soared past the handkerchief, landing 8 1/4 inches beyond it. This astounding leap was not equaled for 25 years. After such a performance, Owens then took his coach's advice and chose not to try for a longer distance.

Immediately, autograph seekers and reporters mobbed the new champion. Owens posed for photographers, shook hands, and signed his name all the way back to the dressing room. So many well-wishers crowded the door there that he had to escape through a back window. In the parking lot, patiently

Owens leaps over a hurdle while training at Ohio State University. Though hurdles were his weakest event, he won the 220-yard competition at the Big Ten Championships in Ann Arbor, Michigan, on May 25, 1935.

waiting in that old Model T, sat Coach Charles Riley, who had cheered with everyone else as Owens rewrote the record books.

As they took the long drive back to Riley's house for a celebratory dinner, the old coach quietly prepared his protégé for the fame that was to come. He explained that life would be different from now on. Owens had been a contender; but in one day he had become a star. Now the top runners in the world would be gunning for him. Fans would surround him. Every move he made would be scrutinized by the press.

No doubt the young runner listened respectfully to Riley's thoughtful advice. Neither man could have guessed that the success they had cultivated for so long would soon be challenged from four different directions. Although none of these challenges came on the track, any one of them might have ended Owens's drive toward the Olympics.

The first challenge arrived in the beautiful person of Quincella Nickerson, a wealthy socialite who took the runner's arm one night in June 1935 after a meet in Los Angeles. Soon images of the glamorous couple were appearing in the local papers, captioned with hints of a wedding engagement.

Ruth Solomon caught up with Owens by telephone when the track team reached Lincoln, Nebraska. While the words they exchanged are not known, what is clear is that the next day, July 4, Owens lost all his races at the AAU Championships. Then he caught the first train back to Cleveland. In the Solomons' living room, which had been off limits to him for so long, he and Ruth were married that afternoon. The event was covered in newspapers nationwide. The next morning, a chastened young husband, still burning from his first brush with celebrity, left for the East Coast and the relative peace and quiet of track meets there.

Shaken by it all, Owens lost his races to a fine runner named Eulace Peacock. Then he returned home to his new family and his summer job at the filling station, reading in the papers that Peacock now seemed to be the front-runner in the race for the Olympics.

PRESSURE AND POLITICS

AAU officials called Owens back to Columbus in August, threatening to bar him from competition. He had received

Jesse Owens and Ruth Solomon were married in the Solomon family living room on July 5, 1935. Owens had become a celebrity after his performance at the Big Ten Championships in May, and his wedding was covered in newspapers nationwide.

checks totaling $159 during the summer from his page's job at the State House. Part of the sum was for travel expenses, and Owens had used the money to pay for his trip to California. To the AAU, the job seemed suspiciously like a cover-up for an outright athletic scholarship. Owens gave back the money, but it took all the persuasiveness of Ohio State University administrators and Ohio lawmakers to convince the AAU to drop its charges.

When his junior year got underway, Owens received yet another slap in the face. Those same university officials who had argued his case so convincingly just weeks before now suspended him from the track team for the winter season. The reason? Poor grades. They threatened to cut the world-record holder in six events from the team unless he hit the books hard.

If that was not enough, world politics impinged on the young runner, too. The Olympic Games were scheduled to begin in less than a year, in Berlin, Germany. Stories had begun to circulate about German mistreatment of Jews, blacks, Catholics, and political dissidents. Many of the nation's leading newspapers were calling for an American boycott of the Olympics in protest of Adolf Hitler's discriminatory policies, and the AAU made a tentative decision to keep American athletes out of the games.

All that winter, as Owens, unable to compete with his teammates, trained on his own, he could not be sure if he would be granted the opportunity to achieve his grand dream of reaching the Olympics. Worst of all, there was nothing he

DID YOU KNOW?

Jesse Owens almost didn't make it to the 1936 Olympics in Berlin, the games that would place him among the greatest American athletes ever. The president of the American Athletic Union, Judge Jeremiah T. Murphy, was alarmed by rumors of persecution of Jews in Nazi Germany and called for a boycott of the games. His was one of many calls for a boycott around the world. An alternative competition, called the People's Olympics, was scheduled to take place in Barcelona, Spain, but was cancelled when the Spanish Civil War erupted.

In the end, U.S. Olympic officials narrowly voted in favor of sending the American athletes to Berlin to compete. Judge Murphy resigned as president and was replaced by Avery Brundage, who made an inspection of Berlin prior to the Olympics and announced that there would be no problems with Americans competing in Nazi Germany.

could do about it. The decision would be made by men in business suits, far from the playing fields.

It must have been a terrible time for the 20-year-old Owens, who faced pressure from all sides—but he remembered the teachings of Coach Riley—to challenge himself, to do his best—and he concentrated on those tasks that were within his control. Gradually, his grades came up, and by the time Owens rejoined the track team for the spring season he had run himself into the best shape of his life.

Against the University of Wisconsin on May 16, just 10 weeks prior to the Olympic Games, Owens ran the 100-yard dash in 9.3 seconds, breaking the world record. While his archrival Eulace Peacock struggled with a hamstring injury, Owens piled up victory after victory, all leading to the Olympic Trials in New York City on June 11 and 12. After an agreeable visit with German chancellor Adolf Hitler, AAU officials had decided that it would be all right for American athletes to compete in Berlin after all. The last barrier to Owens's dream had fallen. Now, after what must have seemed the darkest time since his boyhood illnesses in Alabama, the door stood open for him.

At the Olympic Trials, Owens breezed to victory in the 100-meter and 200-meter dashes and in the long jump. His schoolboy pal David Albritton, also a teammate at Ohio State, made the team as a high jumper. Ralph Metcalfe, the 1932 medalist who had beaten Owens in the trials that same year, also gained a berth. These were 3 of the 19 black athletes who would compete for the United States in the 1936 Olympics, four times the number who had made the team four years earlier. The big disappointment: Eulace Peacock. Hampered by his hamstring injury, he finished out of the running at the trials.

The night following the trials, Owens joined the other Olympians at a celebratory feast in Manhattan. There he was surprised and honored to find himself seated beside the legendary baseball slugger Babe Ruth. As Owens later recalled,

Ruth wasted no time in asking, "You gonna win at the Olympics, Jesse?" Owens replied, "Gonna try."

"Everybody tries," Ruth said. "I succeed. Wanna know why?" Owens nodded.

"Because I know I'm going to hit a home run just about every time I swing that friggin' bat. I'm surprised when I *don't!*

The 1936 Olympics

The decision to hold the 1936 Olympics in Nazi Germany may seem difficult to understand in our modern awareness of the extent of Adolf Hitler's plans for his country. It is important to remember that the decision to award the honor of hosting the Olympic Games to Berlin was made in 1931, two years before Hitler and the Nazi Party came to power.

As word of the persecution of Jews in Nazi Germany began to seep out, many in the international community called for a boycott of the Olympics, and for a time it was uncertain whether or not the American athletes would compete in Berlin. The International Olympic Committee opted to keep the Games in Berlin but promised to maintain close supervision of the events, and finally the American team agreed to participate.

In the end, the 1936 Games drew more countries and hosted more athletes than any previous Olympics. Under Hitler's direction, the Berlin events were staged on a massive scale. His Third Reich spent nearly $25 million to build extraordinary facilities, including a 100,000-seat Olympic stadium and a 20,000-seat swimming venue, as well as a modern, comfortable Olympic village for the athletes—the first of its kind and a tradition that would be followed in future Olympics. The city was scrubbed, trees were planted, and all outward signs of anti-Semitic policies were temporarily removed.

The 1936 Games also launched the tradition of the Olympic torch relay, in which the Olympic torch was lit at the Temple of Zeus in Greece and then carried on to the Olympic Stadium in Berlin, passing through 3,000 pairs of hands on its journey. The 1936 Berlin Olympics also were the first to be televised. Closed-circuit televisions broadcast the games onto 28 large screens placed around the streets of Berlin, so that Germans could gather to watch the competitions.

In the end, Hitler's Olympics proved a triumph for German athletes. They won more medals than any other country, earning 89 overall (the United States earned 56); 33 were gold.

And that isn't all there is to it. Because I know it, the pitchers, they know it too."

Owens grinned at the supreme confidence of the baseball hero. He did not fail to recognize the good advice hidden in the blustering anecdote. Sometimes, it is not enough to *want* to win. Sometimes, you have to *know* that you will. Owens took the Babe's advice with him on board the S.S. *Manhattan* when it departed for Berlin three days later. (For additional information about Babe Ruth, enter "Babe Ruth" into any search engine and browse the many sites listed.)

Every kind of distraction awaited Owens during the week-long voyage, from heavy gourmet meals to Hollywood starlets who vied for his arm on the dance floor. To at least one of the Olympians, the distractions proved too much. The beautiful backstroke champion Eleanor Holm Jarrett partied her way to Berlin—and lost her chance to compete when a chaperone discovered her drunk on champagne one morning. Owens was careful to avoid all the premature celebrating. He kept his mind on his destination, performing calisthenics and watching what he ate, while getting to know his fellow Olympians.

There was a lot of time, too, for thinking over all he had been through, for thrilling to the fact that his wildest dream was about to come true. As Pop Riley had said, "Run to beat yourself." As Babe Ruth had suggested, "Know you will win." He would test both of these axioms, to their limit, in the Olympic Games.

5

The Dream Come True

When the Olympic Games began on August 1, 1936, German Chancellor Adolf Hitler had been running his nation for a little more than three years. In that brief amount of time, he had raised the nation from a poor and broken-spirited country, beaten and divided by the Great War of 1914–18 (what is now called World War I), to a position of power in the world. He had put his unemployed countrymen to work building the first superhighways anyone had ever seen. These were broad and straight concrete roads he called autobahns, on which the powerful cars of the 1930s could run flat out, with no speed limit at all.

The skies of Nazi Germany were ruled by enormous hydrogen-filled zeppelins. The most spectacular of these airships, the *Hindenburg*, stretched the length of three football fields and regularly traveled across the Atlantic Ocean carrying passengers in style. The show of size and strength did not end there. All over Germany, people gladly adopted Hitler's strict programs aimed at making the nation's young people well schooled, physically fit, and proud of their country. (For additional information about the *Hindenburg,* enter "Hindenburg" into any search engine and browse the many sites listed.)

Yet this glittering nation of fast highways and fit youngsters was being built at the expense of the livelihood and freedom of millions of its own people. Hitler's dream nation excluded anyone he did not consider a patriotic native of pure Aryan stock. With fanatical and relentless energy he set about promoting a form of national pride that thrived on the oppression of anyone who did not fit that description.

When he had been in office just one month, Hitler ordered the creation of 50 concentration camps to imprison "enemies of the state." Four months later, 27,000 people—mostly Jews and Communists—were being held under brutal conditions in those camps. Gradually, the numbers of those being forced into these camps grew, while thousands of others fled the country in fear.

Astute observers of the strange goings-on in Germany guessed what Hitler was up to. Those autobahns could be used to transport troops quickly and efficiently all over the country. Those zeppelins and the planes being turned out on German assembly lines could be fitted out for wartime purposes almost instantly. All those schoolboys learning to toss balls accurately into hoops positioned on the ground might just as easily have been throwing grenades. Finally, if the Nazis saw fit to drive out or imprison a large part of their own population, who could say what they might do to other nations in a time of war?

Somehow, few people got the point. Maybe Hitler's clampdown on the German press was the reason. Maybe he charmed the world's leaders into trusting him. Maybe it was simply impossible to believe that a nation beaten into the ground in the ugliest war ever fought, scarcely 17 years earlier, could be thirsting for battle again so soon. Whatever the cause, Hitler began to carry out his plans for genocide and world domination with scarcely a whimper from other governments.

In sponsoring the 1936 Olympic Games, he expected another triumph. He invited the world's greatest athletes, the reporters, the statesmen and socialites, right into his nation's capital and dared them to see anything but good.

For Adolf Hitler, merely sponsoring the Olympic Games was not enough. These sporting events supplied an excellent forum where his notions of Aryan supremacy might be tested. Germany had done well at the 1932 Games in Los Angeles, before Hitler's rise to power. The new chancellor had spared no expense to make sure the Germans would come out victorious this time.

POMP AND POLITICS

Red, white, and black Nazi swastika flags were flying from every shop window on June 24, when the U.S. Olympic team came down the S.S. *Manhattan*'s gangway in Bremerhaven, Germany, touching solid ground for the first time in a week. Catching an express train to Berlin, the team marveled at the beauty of the countryside. Berlin itself had been so carefully renovated for the Games that it seemed to sparkle.

The Germans had built a magnificent Olympic Village to house the athletes a few miles west of the city. This idea worked so well that similar villages have been built for every Olympics since then. The Berlin version included comfortable dormitories, a spacious park, a library, a swimming pool, and theaters. Owens roomed with his high school buddy and Ohio State teammate, high jumper David Albritton.

For two weeks, as other competitors arrived from around the world, the American track team worked off its "sea legs" at the practice track in the Olympic Village. Ohio State track coach Larry Snyder was not an official member of the U.S. delegation, but he had traveled to Berlin at his own expense to keep an eye on Owens and Albritton.

It was lucky for Owens that he did. One day, Snyder arrived at the track to find the Olympic coaches trying to change the running style that he, Coach Charles Riley, and Owens had all but perfected over the past several years. Those coaches were trying to alter Owens's effortless gliding run into the powerhouse style they favored, but Snyder stepped in to convince them to leave well enough alone. Owens had lost his track shoes at the Olympic Trials in New York, so Snyder spent days combing the shops of Berlin for a perfect replacement pair.

There was nothing Snyder could do about all the autograph seekers and photographers who constantly surrounded his star. Adolf Hitler may have had a grudge against people from what he considered to be inferior races, but German youngsters were fascinated by the American who held all those world records. Owens, always smiling and happy to oblige, won their hearts with the few German words he had picked up during his stay. He woke up every morning to the sight of curious faces pressed against his dormitory window, yet he handled the fishbowl of celebrity with a down-to-earth sense of humor that belied all the pressure of the upcoming Games.

By the time August 1 arrived, however, he and his teammates were eager to get on with the competition. They marched into the gigantic crater of a stadium to the roar of 100,000 fans and caught their first glimpse of the German chancellor. Hitler

IN HIS OWN WORDS...

The 1936 Olympics changed Jesse Owens's life forever. Almost as it was happening, Owens was aware of how those games had transformed his future:

It dawned on me with blinding brightness. I realized: I had jumped into another rare kind of stratosphere—one that only a handful of people in every generation are lucky enough to know.

stood in uniform and at attention in his flag-draped viewing box, surrounded by Hermann Göring, Albert Speer, and Joseph Goebbels—all names that would become notorious in the war years ahead.

Owens was largely unconcerned with all the pomp and politics. He had come to Berlin to run and jump. The next day he got his chance. If he had any doubts about his physical condition after the voyage overseas, he quickly wiped them away in the 100-meter eliminations. Cold, drizzly rain fell most of the day, making the track slow and muddy. Without a word of complaint, Owens astounded the crowd by equaling his own world record of 10.3 seconds. In his afternoon heat, he lowered that time by a tenth of a second, but because of a following wind the new record was disallowed.

Reassured that he was still at the top of his form, Owens slipped on his sweat suit and spent the rest of the afternoon watching Albritton compete in the high jump. Before the day was over, both Albritton and his American teammate Cornelius Johnson had broken the world record in their event. Johnson squeezed out a victory with a remarkable leap of 2.3 meters (6 feet, 6 1/4 inches). Albritton, having hurt his ankle during the competition, admitted that he was pleased to have won the silver medal. He took it back to his dormitory room that night, where it did not remain alone for long.

THREE SECONDS

The semifinals and finals of the 100-meter race were held the next day. As Owens warmed up for his semifinal heat, a cloudburst sent the spectators scurrying for cover and muddied the track even more. This was the day Owens had lived for. The dream of a lifetime lay within his grasp.

Later, he would philosophize about the oddity of training so many years for an occasion that would be over in mere seconds. To the runner, he said, the race was both shorter and longer than a spectator could imagine: "To a sprinter, the

Jesse Owens takes off running at the 1936 Summer Olympics in Berlin. "It seems to take an eternity," Owens said of the sprint races, "yet is all over before you can think what's happening."

hundred-yard dash is over in *three* seconds, not nine or ten. The first 'second' is when you come out of the blocks. The next is when you look up and take your first few strides to attain gain position. By that time the race is actually about half over. The final 'second'—the longest slice of time in the world for an athlete—is that last half of the race, when you really bear down and see what you're made of. It seems to take an eternity, yet is all over before you can think what's happening."

According to Owens, people assumed that running 100 meters was just a question of speed. Certainly, that was a lot of it. Against world-class competition, however, the big challenge appeared in the last half of the race, when every instinct, all those years of training, and sheer courage were called upon to squeeze out every last drop of speed. This was what Coach Riley had been talking about in all his high school lectures when he said to "race against yourself." To go to the limit in this way was a supreme sporting achievement.

Owens won his semifinal heat easily, in 10.4 seconds. Then, in the 100-meter finals, he burst into the lead at the starting gun and was never challenged. He broke the tape in 10.3 seconds, tying his own Olympic record. Ralph Metcalfe, the Marquette University sprinter who had won two Olympic medals in Los Angeles, finished second, a yard back—but all eyes were on Owens. One British observer marveled, "No sprinter I have ever seen has run in such effortless style. He was in a class above all other competitors; his arms and legs worked in perfect rhythm, and he carried his running right through the tape."

The results of the race were broadcast on loudspeakers all over Berlin, so, as Owens took his victory lap, shouts in and out of the stadium circled with him. The German crowd had found a hero in the college boy from the United States, and for the rest of the Games, wherever he went, the shout went up: "Yesseh Oh-vens! Yesseh Oh-vens!"

On the victory stand that afternoon, Owens's eyes misted over as he bent forward to receive his gold medal and watched the American flag being raised. He had achieved his dream at last. He would remember this as the happiest moment of his whole career.

As was the custom, Jesse Owens bowed to the leader of the host country—Adolf Hitler—from the victory stand. The German chancellor returned a stiff salute, then turned away. When an aide suggested that he invite Owens to his viewing box, Hitler savagely replied, "Do you really think that I will allow myself to be photographed shaking hands with a Negro?"

Whether Owens knew that he had been snubbed or not, he did not have time to be bothered by a racist politician. The next day, the preliminaries of the 200-meter race began. For the fourth day in a row, rain fell—this time as a bus drove the American track team to the stadium. Owens had to wear his sweatshirt to stay warm during his elimination heats, which he won handily. Then, while the other sprinters caught a bus back to the Olympic Village, he tried to stay loose for the afternoon's long-jump competition, swallowing a damp sandwich for lunch.

UNEXPECTED FRIENDSHIP

The 100-meter victory had seemed so easy, but the long jump proved anything but. In fact, Owens barely made it into the finals. Each athlete was given three chances to qualify, which should have been two more than Owens needed. When he ran, still wearing his sweat suit, through the long-jump pit to gauge the steps for his first leap, he was shocked to discover that the judges counted the run-through as his first attempt. Then, when he *did* jump, they said he had committed a foul by stepping over the takeoff board and disqualified the leap.

Now the pressure was on, and suddenly the power of concentration that had helped make Owens such a formidable competitor deserted him. In his autobiography, Owens recalled that this was the most frightening moment of his career: "I fought, fought hard, harder . . . but one cell at a time, panic crept into my body, taking me over."

He credited a German long jumper, Lutz Long, with pulling him back together for his last leap. The German, who had already qualified for the finals, walked over and asked in his best English, "What has taken your goat, Jazze Owenz?" Owens had to smile at that.

The tension broken, Long suggested to Owens that in his third attempt he take his very last step several inches before the end of the takeoff board, thus making sure that he did not overstep the board and become disqualified. Owens thanked him for the advice, and with the old confidence returning, raced down the runway for his jump. Even though he leaped before the end of the takeoff board, where the officials begin their measurements, he landed more than 26 feet away, a new Olympic record. Again, Owens ran over to thank the German.

All afternoon, Owens and Long were locked in head-to-head competition for the long-jump gold medal. The Olympic record broke with each leap. Yet through it all they cheered each other on. The crowd had never seen anything like it. Long stood a few inches taller than Owens. He was the perfect picture of the Aryan superman—blond, blue eyed, with a perfectly proportioned physique. He was not caught up in Hitler's mania for white supremacy, however. Like Owens, he understood that one competes primarily against oneself, and he seemed genuinely grateful to have at last met a man who could drive him on to a better performance.

Lutz Long jumped with a simple, fluid style, his arms thrown high above his head. Owens "ran through" the jump, hitch kicking in midair as Coach Snyder had taught him, to capitalize on his superior speed. With each jump, the crowd erupted in applause. No doubt the Germans wanted their countryman to win, but Owens had already become a crowd favorite, and

Wearing the victor's laurels, Owens salutes the American flag during an Olympic medal ceremony. Despite their head-to-head competition, Owens became fast friends with German runner Lutz Long (right).

for once it was easy to join in the friendly spirit of competition that the two long jumpers shared.

In the final round, Long matched Owens's record. The two smiled and shook hands. Then Owens went to the board and jumped even further. More applause. Eventually, Long faltered, overrunning the board. A groan went up around the stadium.

With the gold medal awaiting him, Owens gathered himself for one more jump. With confidence and concentration, he sailed to a new Olympic record of 26 feet, 5 5/16 inches. Lutz Long was the first to congratulate Owens, giving him a hearty bear hug in full view of Adolf Hitler.

That evening at the Olympic Village, Owens and Long were inseparable. Though Owens could not speak German and Long knew only a little English, they talked for hours. It turned out that Long had come from a poor family, too. Like Owens, he had a wife and child at home. They spoke about their love for their sport, which offered challenges nothing else could match, and fretted together over racial prejudice in Germany and the United States. By the time the Olympic Games ended, the two had become firm friends. As their relationship was portrayed in newspapers worldwide, they came to represent the way supposed rivals can overcome their differences. Beyond all of Hitler's flag-waving and speeches, the image of Jesse Owens and Lutz Long shaking hands became the over-riding symbol of the 1936 Olympics.

Owens awoke the next day to more rain. He breezed through his semifinal heat in the 200 meters, then spent the afternoon watching Americans Ken Carpenter and Earle Meadows win gold medals in the discus and pole vault, respec-tively. Then, just before sunset, in the 200-meter finals, Owens again proved himself the world's fastest human. On top of all his tutoring by Coaches Riley and Snyder, he had developed a trick or two of his own over the years. One of these accounted in part for his quick takeoffs at the starting gun. Out of the corner of his eye he watched the starter, knowing that there was usually some telltale sign just as the trigger was pulled, and that sign gave Owens a slight jump on his competitors. This technique worked well in Berlin, where the starter habitually bobbed his knees just before pulling the trigger.

Owens knew he would need all his skill to win the 200-meter race. After he had set a new Olympic record of 21.1 seconds in his preliminary heat, teammate Mack Robinson equaled that mark later in the morning. Yet Robinson could not keep up with Owens in the final. Owens held a slight lead coming out of the turn, and when he reached the tape Robinson trailed him by nearly five yards. Owens's time of 20.7 seconds set a new world record for a 200-meter race around a curve. The crowd had barely finished shouting its approval when the skies opened again. Owens received his third gold medal during a downpour.

A CONTROVERSIAL CHANGE

At last, the competition had ended for Owens. He could spend the remaining days in Berlin rooting for his American team-mates, enjoying performances by circus animals, dance troupes, and even the Berlin Philharmonic at the Olympic Village, or trying to make out the shadowy images of other athletes on a prototype television set.

Then the U.S. coaches called him to a meeting. They believed the Germans were saving their best runners for the 400-meter relay race, and for that reason they wanted Owens to run the first leg for the American team. Ralph Metcalfe would run the second leg, virtually assuring an American victory in the event. It is not difficult to imagine the anger of sprinters Marty Glickman and Sam Stoller, who had been slated to run the relay, when they were told that they were being bumped from the race. Owens also seemed surprised. He told the coaches he had enough gold medals and to let the others run.

The coaches would not budge. Glickman and Stoller, the only Jewish members of the U.S. Olympic team, thus became the only two team members who did not compete at the Games. By making the change, U.S. officials seemed suspiciously close to the racist notions that fueled the Nazi government. Their decision fueled suspicion that anti-Semitism was not simply a German problem.

When race day came, Owens, of course, did his best. He handed the baton to Metcalfe with a five-yard lead. Foy Draper started his leg ahead by 7 yards, and Frank Wykoff, who took the baton 10 yards in the lead, lengthened it to 12 by the end of the race. The Americans set a new world record of 39.8 seconds. The Italians won the silver medal, and the Germans came in third. The rumor of a German superteam had amounted to nothing.

Jesse Owens had won his fourth gold medal, an unprecedented feat by a track athlete. He had broken Olympic records in all four events. This achievement overreached his wildest dreams and made him a hero to sports fans worldwide.

One of those fans proved to be Hitler's handpicked cinematographer, Leni Riefenstahl. She filmed the entire 1936 Olympic Games in a sweeping, lyrical style that highlighted the beauty of each event while downplaying all the hoopla over winners and losers. Jesse Owens was her athletic ideal. In her filming of the 100-meter competition, her cameraman zoomed in on Owens's thigh, neglecting all the other runners to show his perfectly toned muscles in action.

Similarly, her portrayal of the Owens–Long duel in the long jump centers on the soaring grace of their leaps, not on their battle for the gold. Riefenstahl's film, *Olympiad*, is sometimes shown on television, especially during Olympic years, and it is easy for a viewer to be drawn into her awe at the magnificence of athletic achievement and particularly at the seemingly effortless beauty of Jesse Owens in full flight.

As the Americans packed their bags at the Olympic Village, they already looked forward to the next Games. These were to be held in Tokyo, Japan, in 1940, when Owens would be just 26 years old. Certainly, he would be back to compete again.

The Germans had goals other than sports in mind. A wooden peg in the closet of each dormitory room had been placed there to hold a helmet. Already in the fields near the Olympic Village machine-gun practice could be heard. The village would become an infantry training center as soon as the athletes departed.

World War II would put an end to any talk of a 1940 or a 1944 Olympics. The German swastika flag would become a hated emblem to people all over the world. As Owens carefully packed his four gold medals for the trip home, he could not

Leni Riefenstahl

Hitler selected cinematographer Leni Riefenstahl to film the 1936 Olympics. The resulting film, *Olympiad*, contains sweeping, lyrical footage of the Games, a four-hour epic focusing less on the winners and losers than on the beauty of the athletic form.

Riefenstahl made several films for Hitler, including *Victory of Faith*, showing the Nazi Party's 1933 Nuremberg rally, in 1934, and the monumental feature-length film *The Triumph of the Will*, coverage of the spectacle that was Hitler's choreographed 1934 Nazi rally, also held in Nuremberg. Her ability to portray such political subjects in sweeping, grand images led critics to charge that Riefenstahl created not cinematography but propaganda.

For the rest of her career, Riefenstahl refuted this criticism and the allegation that she was a supporter of the Nazis. In an interview with the BBC, Riefenstahl explained that her focus was always on making "a film that was not stupid like a crude propagandist newsreel, but more interesting. . . . It reflects the truth as it was then, in 1934. It is a documentary, not propaganda."

Riefenstahl was born in Berlin in 1902 and studied painting before launching a career as an actress and dancer. She both acted in and directed 1932's *Blue Light*, the film that first brought her to Hitler's attention.

After World War II, Riefenstahl's filmmaking career stalled. She turned instead to photography, earning critical acclaim for her photographs of Sudan's Nuba tribe as it battled extinction. Later, she studied diving in order to pursue work as an underwater photographer, and in 2002 she released the acclaimed film *Impressions Under Water*, the result of more than 200 dives.

Riefenstahl died in Poecking, Germany, on September 8, 2003, a few weeks after celebrating her 101st birthday.

have known that he would never compete at another Olympics. He would never again see his new friend Lutz Long either. Like Owens's relay-race teammate Foy Draper, Long would die in a foxhole during the war. (For additional information about World War II, enter "World War II" into any search engine and browse the many sites listed.)

6

After the Gold Rush

What does a 22-year-old do when he has achieved his wildest dream? As the possibilities piled up following his Olympic victories, Jesse Owens could not have guessed that this question would torment him for the rest of his life. It had been one thing to aim his formidable talents at the single goal represented by those five interlocked Olympic hoops. Testing himself against the constantly shifting demands of the non-Olympic world would prove a far more difficult challenge.

Coach Larry Snyder wasted no time in coming to Owens's aid. He arrived in the athlete's room the evening following the 400-meter relay race for a private, man-to-man talk. He had not come to discuss race strategy or running form—none of that mattered anymore—but to consider how Owens might best capitalize on his Olympian achievements. At that moment, it seemed there were two options: return to Ohio

The conquering hero: Wearing the Olympic laurel wreath and a big smile, Jesse Owens displays the three gold medals that he won for his individual prowess in the 1936 Olympics.

State to complete his degree, or drop out of school to make some money from his newfound celebrity.

Even though Owens was the unparalleled star of the school's track team, Coach Snyder was a practical man, and he knew that offers would soon come pouring in, proposing huge amounts for Owens's services. As the Olympic star told a reporter the next morning, "I'm anxious to finish my college career, but I can't afford to miss this chance if it really means big money. I can always go back and get a degree."

Even before Owens had his bags packed, the offers began to arrive. A California orchestra wired him that it would pay him $25,000 just for introducing songs onstage for 2 weeks. Entertainer Eddie Cantor wanted to share a vaudeville stage with Owens, proposing a $40,000 fee for 10 weeks of work. Paramount Pictures talked of a movie deal.

All those zeros made the runner's head spin. To a depression-era American, the sums seemed astronomical. All Owens wanted to do was get home, show those medals to his family, and rest a while before sorting out the opportunities.

The AAU and the U.S. Olympic Committee had other plans. In order to pay team expenses, they had set up post-Olympic track meets all over Europe, and Owens was to be their star gate attraction. Exhausted from a week of record-breaking performances, he had to join his teammates on a trip to Dresden, then on to Cologne and Prague, and back to Bochum, Germany, staging track-and-field exhibitions at each stop. Not surprisingly, the team performed unevenly. If Owens equaled his world record in the 100-meter dash in one city, he lost out to an unknown athlete in the long jump elsewhere.

By the time the team boarded a plane for London, they were homesick, tired, and flat broke. Coach Snyder, angry at the shoddy treatment the AAU was showing some of the world's best athletes, called a stop to it right there. After a meeting with university officials, he announced that Owens was simply too tired to go on. He would run one last time in London and then board a ship for New York.

At the London meet, the American team trounced all comers. Owens, however, competed only on the 400-meter relay team. The 90,000 spectators who had come to see the

Olympic stars perform could not have known that they were witnessing the last amateur race Owens would ever run.

Thanks to the arrogance of AAU officials, that is what happened. Avery Brundage and the other businessmen who ran the U.S. Olympic team were not about to lose their star athlete in the midst of such a lucrative tour—at least not without a fight. They told Snyder to make sure Owens caught the plane to the next meet in Stockholm, or else. When Owens failed to board that plane, the outraged officials suspended him indefinitely from amateur competition. Never mind that the entire world knew about his exploits a week earlier on the track in Berlin. Never mind that he was a hero to people everywhere. The AAU was determined to punish its greatest athlete, simply for wanting to go home.

A HERO'S WELCOME

At least the suspension freed Owens to do what he wanted: He caught the next ship back to the States. Aboard the *Queen Mary* he relaxed, danced, and regained the 10 pounds he had lost during the stress of the Olympics. By the time he arrived in New York four days later, he felt rejuvenated and ready to face the hero's welcome awaiting him.

What a hero's welcome it was. Owens's family was brought out on a launch to meet the ship even before it docked in New York harbor. The women smothered him with kisses. Then, at the dock, Owens answered the questions of clamoring reporters until the great entertainer Bill "Bojangles" Robinson rescued him and his family for a fast-moving motorcade to Harlem. At Robinson's home, Owens found himself the guest of honor of the city's black luminaries, who seemed as eager to shake his hand as the German schoolchildren had been.

Finally, when the party died down, Robinson took Owens aside and introduced the athlete to his show-business agent, Marty Forkins. The agent and the performer had taken sprinter Eddie Tolan under their wing following his victory at the Los Angeles Olympics, and they said they would now be happy to guide Owens through the strange waters of celebrity. His mind spinning with their talk of a Hollywood fortune, Owens gathered his family to catch a train back to Cleveland and the well-deserved rest he had dreamed of ever since he left Berlin.

Owens's hometown fans could not let him rest without first getting a glimpse of their hero. A motorcade wound its way through Cleveland's East Side ghetto and through the fanciest streets in town on its way to welcoming speeches at City Hall. Then it was on to Columbus for another victory procession and more speeches. Finally, three weeks after leaving the Olympics, Owens got a chance to sleep in his own bed.

He was up the next day to haggle with Coach Snyder and Ohio State administrators over what he would do next. Everyone agreed that his best bet at cashing in on his fame was to sign an agency agreement with Forkins. He could always get his college degree later.

So Owens climbed back on the train for New York. While in Manhattan, he met his Olympic teammates as they arrived from Europe, and he rode in the first car of the ticker-tape parade up Broadway that honored their return. Once again, Bill "Bojangles" Robinson was waiting for him. At the final ceremony, held on nearby Randall's Island that afternoon, Owens showed his gratitude to his new friend by giving him one of the gold medals he had won in Berlin.

With all the victory parades out of the way, Owens sat back and waited to pick his way through the many job offers he had received. Then, one by one, before his eyes, they all disappeared. Eddie Cantor backed out of his promise to take Owens on tour, as did the California orchestra that had sounded so eager in Berlin. All the talk of movie deals faded away, too. As Owens remembered years later, "After I came home from the 1936 Olympics with my four medals, it became increasingly apparent that everyone was going to slap me on

Owens poses with his wife, Ruth, aboard the ship that carried them from the Olympics in Berlin to New York. On his arrival, Owens answered clamoring reporters until Bill "Bojangles" Robinson, a popular entertainer, swept Jesse and his family off to his home in Harlem.

the back, want to shake my hand or have me up to their suite. But no one was going to offer me a job."

To make matters worse, the Olympic champion could not compete in track meets anymore. Signing an agency contract had been the last straw for the AAU. Already angry over

Owens's dropping out of the European tour, the organization said that he was now a professional and was therefore ineligible to compete as an amateur ever again.

What was Owens to do now? He did the one thing he knew how to do best: He ran. This time he was running from a banquet to a radio broadcast to a clothing or food endorsement and back to another banquet, earning $1,000 or so at each stop. Any offer Forkins dug up, Owens took. In the months following his return from Berlin, Owens traveled all over the United States, trading his fame for whatever money he could make. No single job amounted to much, but all together they added up to a small fortune.

Before the year was out, Owens had bought his parents a big house, his wife an expensive wardrobe and jewelry, and himself a new Buick sedan. He even took Charles Riley to an auto showroom, trading in that old Model T for a new Chevy. When the Republican Party asked Owens to campaign for its presidential candidate, Alf Landon, Owens balked at first, saying he did not care much about politics. When they reminded him that President Franklin D. Roosevelt, the Democratic candidate in the 1936 presidential race, had not even sent a telegram of congratulations following his Olympic victories, Owens changed his mind. Now he was running the political race, too. At whistlestops all over America, Owens used the speech-making skills he had learned at Ohio State, telling charming anecdotes about his experiences in Berlin and ending each talk with a few words in support of Landon. For this, he earned somewhere between $10,000 and $15,000. All of Owens's public-speaking skills could not help Landon, however. He lost to Roosevelt in a landslide, carrying only two states, Vermont and Maine.

HORSE RACING

Owens was determined to make a living no matter how he had to do it, and he poured all of his athletic intensity into the project. If no one wanted to hire a black Olympic champion, then he would get along as well as he could. When Forkins offered him the opportunity to race in Cuba on the day after Christmas, 1936, Owens reluctantly agreed to pass up the holiday at home. The race was supposed to be against Cuba's fastest sprinter, Conrado Rodriques. The AAU, watching every move Owens made, warned Rodriques that by racing against a professional he risked his own amateur standing.

Owens arrived in Havana on Christmas Day only to learn that the race would not go off as scheduled. The fast-talking promoter, however, said he had something else in mind that might work. He asked if Owens would be willing to run against a horse. At first, Owens must have thought this was a joke. Did the promoter know that he had learned to run from watching horses race? What was he to do? He was in Cuba at Christmas, the money was on the table. Owens reluctantly agreed.

The race took place at halftime of a soccer game. To make matters worse, when Owens jogged onto the field rain came pouring down. Only 3,000 fans remained in the stands. There at the starting line was his competition, jockey J.M. Contino, astride the thoroughbred Julio McCaw. Owens later said that he felt sick at that moment, realizing what he was about to do. He went through with it. He lined up with a 40-yard head start and raced 100 yards further down the field, beating the

IN HIS OWN WORDS...

The experience of racing thoroughbred horse Julio McCaw during the halftime of a soccer game in Cuba humiliated Owens. Even years later, the experience left him slightly bitter:

It was bad enough to have toppled from the Olympic heights to make my living competing with animals. But the competition wasn't even fair. No man could beat a race horse, not even for 100 yards.

horse by several steps. Then he took the $2,000 payment and went home.

It did not escape Owens's notice how far he had fallen in just four months since the Olympic Games. He was at that moment one of the most famous people in the world, and newspapers everywhere carried photographs of his race against the horse. Some even quoted Owens, saying how good it felt to be out running again. If fans were dismayed at their hero's misfortune, Owens had never been one to complain— and if racing against horses or campaigning for a politician would help support his family, he would do it again.

This is how, in the weeks following his Olympic triumph, Jesse Owens set the stage for the rest of his life.

7

Barnstormin'

The only person who came through on his promise to help Jesse Owens after the 1936 Olympics was Bill "Bojangles" Robinson. The veteran showman fitted the runner out in a white suit and tails, briefed him on holding the attention of a nightclub audience, and helped him win a whopping $100,000 contract to lead a 12-piece black touring band. Ruth Owens was now expecting her second child. She had just picked out a new house in Cleveland and was busy decorating. She would have to make that house a home by herself, because in January 1937 her famous husband hit the road.

Years later, Owens would laugh while describing to William O. Johnson, Jr., author of *All That Glitters Is Not Gold: The Olympic Games,* his months as a bandleader: "Well, I couldn't play an instrument. I'd just stand up front and announce the numbers. They had me sing a little, but that was a horrible mistake. I can't carry a tune in a bucket. We played black

In January 1937, Consolidated Radio Artists sought to capitalize on Owens's fame by offering him the position of bandleader of a 12-piece orchestra. The music company reportedly paid him $100,000, making it one of the most lucrative deals Owens ever made.

theaters and nightclubs all over hell. One-nighters. Apollo Theater in Harlem and the Earle Theater in Philly—that was big time for blacks."

Sometimes, Owens would scout out the town he awoke in, and if a baseball game was scheduled there, he would cut a deal for a running exhibition between innings. It was a grueling life, fights often broke out on the dance floors, and Owens missed his family. Finally, he came down with strep throat in Richmond, Virginia, and called it quits, giving up that huge contract for a chance to spend time at home and to get to know his baby daughter, Marlene.

At that time, freewheeling basketball teams toured the country, dazzling the locals with their prowess. Today, the Harlem Globetrotters are the last of these teams to survive, but in the fall of 1937, when Owens formed a team of Cleveland hotshots he named the Olympians, there were similar groups all over. Owens went out on the road with this crew, which played in large and small towns across America. Before spring came, the Olympians had played 142 games, winning all but 6. As an added attraction, Owens often ran exhibition races at halftime. When the season ended, the team had barely broken even, and Owens returned home looking for new money-making ventures.

He hired some of the same players for a barnstorming softball team called the Olympics and traveled with them on weekends in the summer. By now, though, he was finding it difficult to pay his debts, especially the notes on his and his parents' new homes. Coach Riley discovered to his dismay that Owens had covered only the down payment on his Chevy, and Riley had to struggle on his teacher's salary to make the monthly payments.

So Owens decided to get a job. At just over $1,000 for the summer, his position as a bathhouse attendant for Cleveland's recreation department was a far cry from his stipend as a bandleader, but at least it helped pay the bills. Before the summer ended, he had parlayed that job into a better-paying position as a playground director.

Still, those legs that had run so far were not ready to quit yet. For the grand opening of nighttime baseball at Ebbetts Field in Brooklyn, New York, Owens showed up to race against the fastest athletes baseball had to offer. At another game in Chicago later that summer, he challenged heavyweight boxing champion Joe Louis to a 60-yard sprint.

Owens raced against horses, too, learning after a while a few circus tricks to make it easier. As he told William O. Johnson, Jr., "The secret is, first, get a thoroughbred horse because they are the most nervous animals on earth. Then get the biggest gun you can find and make sure the starter fires that big gun right by that nervous thoroughbred's ear." By the time the jockey got his mount settled down, Owens would be halfway down the track. Still, the races were close.

For Owens, it would never be enough just to hold a job, run a baseball team, and tour as a runner-for-hire. Before long, he had started a dry-cleaning business as well. The first of these establishments opened on Cleveland's East Side, where Owens had grown up. The sign out front read, "Speedy 7-Hour Service by the World's Fastest Human." Constantly on the road, Owens left the dry cleaning to business partners and signed on to tour for a while with a team of baseball-playing comedians aptly named the Indianapolis Clowns.

Owens had never been much of a ballplayer, however. He later said that his role came at the end of the game, as the grand finale: "We'd get into these little towns and tell 'em to get out the fastest guy in town and Jesse Owens'd spot him ten yards and beat him." This is why there are old men all over America still telling yarns about racing against Jesse Owens. Many of them actually did.

Maintaining all of these ventures at the same time eventually proved too much for Owens. All at once, the whole world seemed to come crashing down. It started when the Internal Revenue Service demanded payment for back taxes. Owens lost the dry-cleaning business trying to pay that debt. Then, in March 1940, his beloved mother, Mary Emma, his first and greatest inspiration, died at the age of 64. In a car crash that summer, Owens's Buick was totally destroyed. He escaped with a few bruises, but the brush with death was terrifying. As a final blow, his world record in the 220-yard low hurdles fell, another sign of his mortality. When his third daughter, Beverly, was born, Owens realized it was time to take stock of where he was headed.

BACK TO COLLEGE

Owens made the courageous choice to start from scratch. In the fall of 1940, he returned to Ohio State to get his degree.

In the fall of 1940, Owens (left) returned to Ohio State University with the hope of earning his college degree. He helped pay for his tuition by assisting Larry Snyder as coach of the track team.

Even though the AAU still refused to allow him to compete as an amateur, Coach Larry Snyder gladly hired him to help with the track team. Owens's entire family moved to Columbus, and he settled into the life of a student.

Yet as hard as he tried, the 27-year-old college junior could not make it work. In September, his father died of a heart attack. Owens mourned while sweating over the tough required courses he had postponed during his glory years. Finally, he had to face the fact that he would never get a diploma. In December 1941, halfway through his second year back in school, he called it quits. His average on a 4.0 scale was just 1.07.

That same month, the Japanese bombed the Pearl Harbor naval base in Hawaii, and the United States entered World War II. Because he was the head of a household, Owens was not drafted into military service, but the government nevertheless found a role for him at home. The Civilian Defense Office put Owens in charge of a national physical fitness organization. For a year, he toured the country setting up exercise programs at black schools and community halls.

Then Owens was offered the best job he would ever hold. Ford Motor Company, which was turning its assembly lines into military factories for the war effort, hired him as a personnel officer for its thousands of black workers in Detroit. This was the perfect job for a man with limitless energy, prestige, and a way of getting along with almost anybody.

Owens started out by mediating difficulties that came up between the company and the United Auto Workers of America union. By the time the war ended, Owens had expanded his position so that he was helping black workers find better housing, establishing recreation facilities in their neighborhoods, and welcoming new immigrants to the Motor City. At last, he had found work that allowed him to use his talents in a way that not only paid his rent but helped others as well. Not since he had thrilled the crowds at the Olympics had he felt this good.

When the Germans, and then the Japanese, surrendered in 1945, Owens had to surrender his job as well. With Ford restructuring itself to make cars again, many of the wartime managers, including Owens, were dismissed.

THE WORLD'S FASTEST SPOKESPERSON

He went back to his old barnstorming ways, touring for a while with the Harlem Globetrotters. At an exhibition in Milwaukee in 1950, at the age of 37, he ran a 100-yard dash in the astounding time of 9.7 seconds, less than half a second off his own world record. One wonders what feats he might have accomplished had the Olympic Games been held during the interim. He could not go on like that forever. Besides, he had caught a glimpse of another way of life during his years at Ford. Jesse Owens would never be one to stay put for long, but in his remaining years he would find a way to combine his need to constantly keep moving with the opportunity to make more money than he had ever imagined earning.

The key was public relations. As American companies grew larger and more powerful in the years after World War II, they spent more money on advertising and on making themselves look good to their customers. Olympic hero Jesse Owens, the first American to put Hitler in his place, seemed the perfect choice to promote their goods.

Today, of course, when athletes and rock stars advertise all sorts of products at every opportunity, public relations of this sort is commonplace. At that time, however, during the infancy of television, companies were just beginning to recognize the advantages of having a celebrity sell their wares.

Owens became the self-admitted prototype of the "famous flack." In Chicago, where he moved his family in 1949, he held public relations positions for clothing factories, insurance companies, and dry cleaners while plugging a variety of other products on television and radio. He was so swamped with offers that he had to form his own public relations firm to keep track of them all. Fourteen years after his Olympic triumph, some of the reward for his toil in Berlin had begun to come through.

As he recalled in his autobiography, however, it all just meant more work: "People who worked with me or knew me still called me the 'world's fastest human' because I almost never stopped. I'd found that I could get more done with no regular job or regular hours at all, but by being on my own, flying to speak here, help with a public relations campaign for some client there, tape my regular jazz radio show one morning at 5:00 A.M. before leaving on a plane for another city or another continent three hours later to preside over a major sporting event."

Owens's barnstorming days were over. Never again would he have to race against a horse or some cocky local yokel to make ends meet.

8

A Patchwork Quilt

Jesse Owens's second wave of fame began in 1950, when the Associated Press named him the greatest track-and-field athlete in history. He was given the award at a huge banquet in Chicago, where he then lived, attended by 600 business leaders and sportsmen. Owens's acceptance speech sounded a lot like the other speeches he had been giving for years. He reminisced about his rough childhood, used his memory of German long jumper Lutz Long to demonstrate how even enemies can overcome their differences, and swore by the difficult lesson he had learned over the past several years—that with hard work, even a poor boy can make good in America.

This was exactly what the business leaders wanted to hear. These were the years of the cold war with the Soviet Union, when Communism became a dirty word in the United States and many people were hounded from their jobs for not seeming patriotic enough. Almost overnight, Jesse Owens became

Owens leaps down the stairs of the Waldorf Astoria. He had been invited to attend a dinner for the All Time, All Star United States Olympic track and field team, for which he had been selected by national vote among sportswriters, radio and television representatives.

a symbol of the "American way of life." It was not that he was saying anything differently than he ever had before; it was just that now those words readily blended in with the mood of the country. A registered Republican ever since his ill-fated campaign for Alf Landon in 1936, Owens soon became a favorite of Republican President Dwight D. Eisenhower.

While corporations scrambled to get Owens to endorse their products, the president sent him overseas as a goodwill representative of the government. On one of these tours, when he traveled through Berlin, he met the son of his long-lost friend Lutz Long. It was the youngster who broke the news to Owens that Long had been killed in the trenches during the war. Just as he had done with the long jumper years before, Owens talked with the young man late into the night.

Back in Chicago, Owens joined the board of directors of the South Side Boys Club, where he personally organized programs to help out troubled youngsters in the city's black ghetto. Appointed chairman of the Illinois State Athletic Commission, he worked hard to promote athletics as a way out of poverty for poor youngsters. Meanwhile, he kept up his usual schedule of publicity appearances and radio shows, somehow finding time to tour the Far East as a goodwill ambassador for the State Department. This was a backbreaking schedule, and it would only accelerate in the years ahead.

Gradually, as Owens raced from airport to airport, he began to tire of it all. He wrote, "I was getting to be just another old jockstrap. . . . Maybe I was fur-lined, but I was still a jockstrap." When his long-standing world records in the 100-yard dash and 400-meter relay fell, that feeling hit him

IN HIS OWN WORDS...

In November 1970, Owens traveled to Reading, Pennsylvania, to speak to a group of nearly 800 teachers and administrators at the Reading School District. He urged those gathered to understand how athletics could be a stepping-stone for those seeking to escape poverty. His comments, printed in the December 1, 1970, *Times* of Reading, reflect a man who has carefully considered the highs and lows of his career.

I wouldn't want to change anything in my life, and there's nothing else I'd rather be doing now. Sure, I've had ups and downs, but God has been very good to me. If I had a pencil and eraser and could start over again, I couldn't improve anything.

harder. Jesse Owens was 43 years old now. His daughter Marlene had just enrolled at his alma mater, Ohio State University. Yet he had to admit to himself that he still had not found anything to compare with the youthful thrill of those Olympic Games so long ago.

He never would. One by one, his world records fell, the last being his long-jump mark, which American Ralph Boston overtook at the 1960 Olympics in Rome. Interviewed there about his feelings, Owens shrugged and said, "It's like having a pet dog for a long time. You get attached to it, and when it dies you miss it."

That same year, Owens had the haunting experience of appearing on "This Is Your Life," a television show in which celebrity guests won the mixed blessing of being surprised by faces from their past. Coach Charles Riley, old and feeble by now, made the trip from his retirement home in Sarasota, Florida, to Los Angeles for the show. It dawned on Owens that he had not taken the time to see his old mentor in 15 years. This was the last time the two would meet. Riley died a few months later.

Owens was aware, too, that he hardly knew his family. All three of his daughters were grown and gone. His wife, Ruth, had done what she could to make a good family life for them all, but with his schedule of constant travel, Owens had spent little time at home. Yet he found it impossible to stop, or even slow down.

1968 OLYMPICS

Owens campaigned for Richard Nixon in 1960 in a losing presidential battle against John F. Kennedy, and in 1965 he joined the hapless New York Mets at their training camp as a running coach. Even a ruptured disk suffered while with the Mets, and the resulting neurosurgery, did not slow him down for long. Meanwhile, the list of products he endorsed grew and grew. His corporate clients included Ford Motor

Company, Sears Roebuck, Atlantic-Richfield, and U.S. Rubber. During the 1968 Olympics, he appeared in television advertisements for Schlitz beer.

It was at those 1968 Olympic Games, held in Mexico City, that this self-professed "old jockstrap" really began to feel the pinch of age. As usual, he arrived at the Games only to be mobbed by throngs of adoring fans. As a paid consultant to the U.S. Olympic Committee, however, he had serious work to do. The year 1968 was one of revolt and upheaval around the world. The civil rights movement and opposition to the Vietnam War raged in the United States, and just one week before the Olympics began hundreds of student demonstrators had been shot and killed by police in Mexico City. To a conservative Republican like Jesse Owens, things seemed out of control.

The great American sprinters that year were Tommie Smith and John Carlos, both students at San Jose State University in California. Tall and powerful, Smith had held 11 world records, and he blazed to a new 200-meter mark of 19.8 seconds in the Olympic final. Carlos won the bronze, finishing less than a step behind. They arrived at the podium to receive their medals barefoot. This was intended as a remembrance of black poverty in the United States. As the American flag rose, they raised their right fists encased in black gloves—a black power salute—and bowed their heads.

This gesture was an elegant example of nonviolent protest, but beamed worldwide by satellite television, it set off a wave of indignation in conservative circles. Jesse Owens, the man whose performance in Berlin had itself seemed a protest against Hitler's racism, was called in to help. He sat down with Smith and Carlos afterward, begging them to apologize. He told them, "The black fist is a meaningless symbol. When you open it, you have nothing but fingers—weak, empty fingers. The only time the black fist has significance is when there's money inside. There's where the power lies." Smith and Carlos looked at this man who had been their hero and realized that more than a generation gap lay between them. They refused to apologize and were promptly kicked off the U.S. Olympic team.

Tommie Smith and John Carlos

Jesse Owens was familiar with how political events can tinge Olympic competition. Nonetheless, he was horrified by the decision of two American athletes to use the 1968 Olympics in Mexico City as a forum for airing their views on the civil rights struggle.

The 1968 Olympics had been marked by controversy. Before the Games began, student protests against the government of Mexican president Gustavo Diaz Ordaz resulted in a massacre on October 2, only 10 days before the opening ceremonies. More than 200 students were killed when soldiers opened fire on the protestors. Hundreds more were injured and thousands were arrested.

Political symbolism firmly took center stage when sprinters Tommie Smith and John Carlos, gold and bronze medalists in the 200-meter Olympic final, stepped onto the podium in bare feet to accept their medals—a gesture intended to symbolize the poverty of American blacks. Later, as the *Star Spangled Banner* was played, Smith and Carlos bowed their heads and raised their right fists, fists on which they wore black gloves. The gesture, known as the "Black Power salute," was intended as a form of protest against racial discrimination in the United States.

Smith and Carlos were teammates at California's San José State College. Their gesture was not spontaneous but instead was prompted by a friend, sociologist Harry Edwards, who had urged black American athletes to boycott the 1968 Olympics to protest racial discrimination. Smith and Carlos decided to attend the Games but agreed to make the gesture if they won medals.

The International Olympic Committee was outraged and evicted the two from the Olympic Village, although they were not stripped of their medals. They returned to the United States, where they encountered hostility and criticism.

Both later found work in the field of education. Carlos served as head of discipline at a California high school; Smith became a college track-and-field coach. In 2001, Smith attempted to sell his gold medal for $500,000, but there were no buyers. Smith was better known for his gesture than for the world record of 19.83 seconds he set during the 200-meter race, but the record held for more than 10 years and was not broken in Olympic competition until 1984.

Owens went home furious. Somehow, he failed to make the connection between their performance in Mexico City and his own in Berlin. With sports writer Paul Neimarck, he dashed off a book entitled *Blackthink: My Life as Black Man and White Man*, determined to show the world that not all black Americans were militants.

Blackthink, which was published in 1970, is a strange book, filled with a middle-aged man's anger and confusion at a changing world. In it, Owens lashes out at the nation's civil rights leaders, calling them complainers and "pro-Negro bigots." Those civil rights leaders found it hard to forgive Owens for his accusations, particularly this line: "If the Negro doesn't succeed in today's America, it is because he has chosen to fail."

Though the mainstream press supported *Blackthink*, angry letters poured into Owens's Chicago home. His barber refused to cut Owens's hair after reading the book. One reader suggested Owens take another look at the nation he had been racing across for 30 years, including with his letter a copy of the angry autobiography *Soul on Ice* by black militant Eldridge Cleaver. Bewildered by the stir he had caused, Owens sat down and read the book. It opened his eyes to the prejudice and hard times faced by many black Americans, difficulties that, because of his fame, he had been able to skirt most of his life.

I HAVE CHANGED

Owens decided to write a new book, *I Have Changed*. Published in 1972, it is his apology for the bullheaded arrogance of *Blackthink*. "I realized now," he wrote, "that militancy in the *best* sense of the word was the *only* answer where the black man was concerned, that any black man who wasn't a militant in 1970 was either blind or a coward."

Owens added, however, that for him militancy did not mean violence, unless violence meant survival. He wanted to carve out a middle ground between conservatives and the youthful militants. He called it the "immoderate moderate." Like many

Americans of his generation at that time, Owens had been shaken by the events of the 1960s and came out on the other side changed.

Eldridge Cleaver

Owens's view of the civil rights struggle would change dramatically when he read *Soul on Ice*, the 1968 book by black militant Eldridge Cleaver that exposed Owens to a raw life spent battling prejudice and poverty. Cleaver, too, would experience a change of viewpoint, a journey that took him from fame as a Black Panther activist to life as a born-again Christian and member of the Republican Party.

Cleaver was born on August 31, 1935, in Wabbaseka, Arkansas. His family moved to Los Angeles when Cleaver was a teenager, and it was there that he became involved in drugs and violence and eventually was arrested for theft and for selling marijuana. In 1957, he was sent to California's notoriously violent San Quentin and Folsom prisons, after a conviction for assault with intent to murder. In prison, Cleaver wrote the essays that became *Soul on Ice*, a harrowing book that recounts Cleaver's controversial plans for revolutionary violence—plans that would form the foundation of the Black Power movement.

After his release from prison in 1968, Cleaver became one of the founders of a militant black nationalist group known as the Black Panthers, based in Oakland, California. The Panthers supported the idea of a violent overthrow of the current political system in America—an approach to civil rights that contrasted starkly with the nonviolent movement espoused by Martin Luther King, Jr. Cleaver served as the group's spokesman.

Cleaver ran for president in 1968, representing the Peace and Freedom Party. Wounded during a gun battle between the Black Panthers and Oakland police, for which he faced criminal charges, Cleaver jumped bail and fled the United States, living in Algeria, Cuba, and France.

Cleaver returned to the United States in 1975 and publicly renounced the Black Panthers. Eventually, the attempted murder charges against him were dropped, and he was placed on probation. Cleaver became a born-again Christian and attempted to run for a Senate seat as a Republican. In the mid-1980s, he became addicted to crack cocaine and again faced criminal charges for burglary and drug possession. Eventually, he was able to overcome his addiction and worked as a consultant on racial issues. He died in April 1998, at the age of 62.

Changed, but not slowed down. Writer William O. Johnson, Jr., caught up with him on a speaking tour in 1971 and saw Owens in full stride: "He is a kind of all-around super-combination of nineteenth-century spellbinder and twentieth-century plastic P.R. man, a full-time banquet guest, eternal glad-hander and evangelistic small-talker. Muted, tasteful, inspirational bombast is his stock in trade."

Owens himself might not have argued with Johnson. In *I Have Changed*, he marveled at the half million miles he traveled each year, listing the events of one average week: "In the space of less than seven days, I attended a track meet in Boston, flew from there to Bowling Green for the National Jaycees, then to Rochester for the blind, Buffalo for another track meet, New York to shoot a film called, 'The Black Athlete,' Miami for Ford Motor Company, back up to New York for 45 minutes to deliver a speech, then into L.A. for another the same night."

For years, Ruth had pleaded with her prosperous husband to slow down and enjoy the wealth he had earned. At last, he agreed to move from the hustle and bustle of Chicago to quieter Scottsdale, Arizona. He was 65 years old now, the age when most workers retire. Yet he could not give up the road and rarely made it home.

The great athlete's health gradually began to fail. In the winter of early 1979, he caught pneumonia—the illness that had haunted his childhood. Then, during a speech in St. Louis, Missouri, a few days after Thanksgiving, 1979, Owens had to suddenly leave the stage. He went to see his doctor in Chicago only to hear two terrifying words: lung cancer. Owens had smoked cigarettes for 30 years, and at last the habit had taxed his lungs past their limit.

The doctors treated Owens all winter, only to see him grow weaker. Still, they often caught him on the telephone, lobbying President Jimmy Carter and American athletic officials in an effort to keep them from boycotting the 1980 Olympic Games, which were to be held in Moscow. He lost out in that effort. American athletes did not compete in the 1980 Olympics. He did not live to hear that news. On March 31, 1980, Jesse Owens died at a hospital in Tucson, Arizona, at the age of 66.

LEGACY OF A CHAMPION

Two thousand people attended Jesse Owens's funeral at Oak Woods Cemetery in Chicago. After his death, Ohio State University announced that a new track complex would bear his name; athletic awards, scholarships, and annual track meets were created in his honor; and monuments were built to him in his childhood hometowns of Oakville, Alabama, and Cleveland, Ohio. A decade after his death, President George H.W. Bush awarded him the Congressional Medal of Honor. Perhaps the greatest of these memorials was the one in Berlin, Germany: The street leading to the Olympic Stadium there was renamed "Jesse Owens Strasse."

In an effort to make sense of his life, Owens wrote in *I Have Changed*, "The lives of most men are patchwork quilts. Or at best one matching outfit with a closet and laundry bag full of incongruous accumulations." Astonishing athlete, advertising man, government emissary—Owens had worn these and many other hats, often at the same time, during his career. Perhaps it was his loss that he never found work that could compare with the athletic challenges of his amateur days, but in the patchwork quilt that he made of his life, he touched millions of people in a way that he never could have by following a single line of work.

Owens always knew, however, that his greatest moment had been at the Berlin Olympics in 1936. That was when he proved himself more than a record-breaking athlete; the world discovered that he was a great sportsman as well. His showdown with Nazi Chancellor Adolf Hitler has grown into a sports legend, but another aspect of the Games is even more significant: Owens's friendly competition with German long jumper Lutz

Pallbearers carry the casket of former Olympic athlete Jesse Owens after his funeral service on April 4, 1980. Standing immediately behind is Reverend Jesse Jackson; an honor guard salutes in the foreground.

Long will forever symbolize the way so-called enemies can work together to discover the best within themselves.

Thanks to the adoring attention of filmmaker Leni Riefenstahl's film *Olympiad*, it will always be possible to share the remarkable electric charge that went through the crowd in Berlin's Olympic Stadium in 1936. On the screen, an athlete like no other bursts from the starting line, instantly moving into an effortless, fluid stride. His feet seem to barely touch the ground. Before the eyes, he sails past all competitors and into the record books. The race, as Jesse Owens himself said, seems to be over in no time at all and yet to last an eternity.

Appendices

Appendix A:
Newspaper articles about
the career of Jesse Owens

Cleveland News
Saturday, May 25, 1935

OWENS SETS 3 WORLD RECORDS
Jumps 26 Ft. 8 1/4 In., Runs 220 in 20.3, and Hurdles in 22.6

By Jack Clowser

Ann Arbor, Michigan–Cleveland's Jesse Owens ascended the all-time pinnacle of the track and field world today, smashing three world records and tying a fourth as he turned the 35th annual Western Conference meet into the greatest one-man athletic show in history.

Here is what the sensational Ohio State sophomore did, in the order of his performances:

- **RACED** 100 yards in 9.4 seconds, tying Frank Wyckoff's world mark.

- **BROAD JUMPED** 26 feet 8 1/4 inches, smashing the world records held by Chuhei Nambu of Japan by 6 1/8 inches.

- **WHIPPED** through the 220-yard dash in 20.3 seconds clipping three-tenths of second off the former world record held by Roland Locke of Nebraska.

- **SPED** over the 220-yard low hurdles in 22.6 seconds, eclipsing the former mark, 23 seconds flat, held jointly by Charley Brookins of Iowa and Norman Paul of Southern California.

It was the second successive week that Owens smashed the world low hurdle mark and the second week in a row he had tied the classic century dash record.

In the light of Owens's incredible feats everything else, including the team title, seemed to fade into insignificance. Never before in the archives of the cinder path has an individual competitor performed in such breathtaking fashion.

Displaying his usual seemingly effortless style in the century, the former Cleveland East Tech flash breasted the finish line five yards ahead of Grieve of Illinois, who took second place as he drove past Sam Stoller of Michigan in the last 10 yards. Every one of the five timers' watches registered a shade under 9.4 seconds but not enough to reach the coveted 9.3 goal which has been prophesied for Owens this season.

New York Herald Tribune
Sunday, January 31, 1960

WORKS TO HELP UNDERPRIVILEGED
Jesse Owens, America's Mr. Olympics of '36, Still a Champion

By Al Laney

During the summer of 1951, the United States High Command in Germany arranged a show in the stadium where Adolf Hitler had made a Nazi festival of the Olympic Games of 1936. Part of the show was put on by the Harlem Globetrotters and part of the Trotters was Jesse Owens, the wonderful Negro athlete from Ohio State who had won four gold medals in this arena.

A crowd of 75,000 turned out. No doubt many of them had been present for the Games and certainly many came from Soviet-occupied East Berlin. It was Owens's job to conduct the between-halves show on the Trotter tour but on this occasion he came onto the platform in a sweat suit such as he had worn between his thrilling performances in 1936 when he had left those deeds to speak for him.

Now, fifteen years later, he took the microphone and spoke to the great crowd. Choosing carefully the words because they were unrehearsed, he addressed them as follows:

SPECIAL WORDS
"Words often fail on occasions like this. But I remember the fighting spirit and sportsmanship shown by German athletes, especially Lutz Long, the man I managed to beat in the broad jump on my last jump.

"Hitler stood right up in that box. But I believe the real spirit of Germany, a great nation, was exemplified down here on the field by athletes like Lutz.

"I want to say to the young people here to be like those athletes. I want to say to all of you to stand fast with us and let us all work together to stay free and God Almighty will help us in our struggle. This is what the United States stands for and I know you are with us. God bless you all."

When he had finished he received from that German crowd the thunderous ovation so long overdue, a roaring salute surpassing anything they had given their own back in the Nazi days. The noise finally died down and Walter Schreiber, the mayor of Free West Berlin advanced toward Owens and said for all to hear:

"Hitler refused to shake your hand. But I give you both hands."

Again the crowd roared.

ENDURING MYTH

It is not irrelevant to recall this dramatic scene although there lies in Herr Schreiber's words a myth that no doubt will endure. Hitler and all the big Nazi figures did attend the games and they did wear an excess of arrogance on their faces, much more than was needed for the occasion. But truth impels one to recall that Hitler did not offer insults to what Joseph Goebbels called "the Black Auxiliaries" and he did not refuse to shake hands. There was, in fact, no occasion when he might have done so.

The report of the insult was at best a misunderstanding and at worst a deliberate distortion for the sake of a headline. It is pertinent to recall these events nearly a quarter century after because of what is happening today but more because of the way in which the principal actor in the drama speaks about them. Jesse Owens sat and talked long on these and related matters.

"Of course I've know all along that there was nothing in that story about Hitler," he said. "But for years every time I'd meet a stranger he'd asked about it. It was taken for granted everywhere and finally I got tired of denying it.

"MAY DO GOOD"

"And you know, when I visited that stadium again, remembering all that really did happen the first time and having to speak to the new crowd full of young people, I suddenly thought what a good thing it might be that the error had become fact. I seemed to feel that it might be wrong to destroy the myth now. Let it stand, I told myself. Let people believe it and it may do some good."

They are the remarks of a sensitive and thoughtful man who has not come hurriedly to the beliefs he holds. And, to give him the understanding he deserves, it would be good to sketch in the background.

Jesse Owens was born in Alabama; he was old enough to have learned what it meant to be a Negro in the South. Then he also learned somewhat the opposite, or how easy things can be for one favored by fortune. He was a brilliant and famous high school athlete and even more brilliant and famous when he got into college.

He was one of the most thrilling performers ever seen on a running track, and there were several occasions when he was sensational. There that day at Ann Arbor in 1935 when he made three world records—220 (20.3); 200 low hurdles (22.6); broad jump (26-81/4), a mark which still stands—and tied another, the 100 in 9.4.

And then on the world stage at Berlin, the greatest possible moment for a track athlete came for him before that huge Nazi crowd of 110,000. There Owens had the marvelous experience of maintaining an absolute peace in the most important week of this life to that time. The wonderful picture of him in those days remains forever in the mind, a sepia streak running with a faultless style so smooth and silken as to suggest flight through the air.

4 OLYMPIC MEDALS

For example, his Olympic victories—10.3 in the 100 meters,

20.7 in the 200 meters, 26-51/4 in the broad jump, and a share in the 440-meter relay—which brought him four gold medals.

These flawless performances and publicity of the supposed insult made Jesse Owens's name known everywhere and when he returned from Europe he decided to gather a few material rewards for himself. For nearly 20 years then he led a varied and unusually interesting life.

He joined with Bill Robinson, the beloved Bojangles, for exhibitions. He ran races against horses and motorcycles, appeared in ball parks, traveled with a jazz band, sold insurance, was a newscaster and sports commentator, went back to Ohio State to do graduate work, and recruited a basketball team in Cleveland and took it on tour.

Then, as war approached, Owens was called by the government to join its physical fitness program, first in Philadelphia and then in Detroit where, eventually, he became a personnel director for the Ford Motor Company. During one of his basketball tours before the war he had met up with Abe Saperstein in Seattle at a time when neither Owens's tour nor that of the Trotters was prospering sensationally. So they joined forces with Owens, taking charge of the show between games of the double headers.

This had been a very good deal for Owens and after the war he rejoined the Trotters. So at last he came to that dramatic moment before the microphone in the Berlin stadium. That association with the Trotters also led him indirectly to the work in which he is now engaged and in which he believes so completely.

First, Owens was approached during a stop in Chicago by a big clothing merchant who wanted to do something for underprivileged youngsters and incidentally also to sell more clothes. Jesse took this job because it revealed to him suddenly what it really was he ought to do and wanted to do. That is, he felt that now he was especially prepared to work with young people.

AID TO YOUTH

After a while he left the clothing store to take over the South Side Boys Club in Chicago and was so successful with this work that he was sent for by William G. Stratton, the present governor of Illinois, who was only hoping to be at that time. With an eye on the South Side vote, the governor offered Jesse a job campaigning and Jesse agreed on condition that Mr. Stratton should write into his platform that, if elected, he would do something about helping the youth of Illinois.

That is how the Illinois Youth Commission was set up, modeled after those in New York and California, and how Jesse Owens, one of four commissioners, came finally to the work he will sit all night to tell you about if you have time and the will to listen.

Jesse makes this work sound immensely important since it helps keep kids of all races and creeds out of mischief and active at constructive things. He works patiently at rehabilitation with those who have got into trouble. He makes himself sound thoroughly dedicated to it and he is completely convincing.

Jesse is 46 now. He getting just a little bald and just a little bulgy here and there, as befits a man who has recently become a grandfather. He has three daughters but no son. One teaches in a Chicago elementary school and is married to a teacher. One is a teller in a Chicago bank and she is the mother of the first grandchild. And the third daughter is in her last year at Jesse's alma mater, Ohio State.

A clear thinker and a fluent talker, Owens seems to feel that all he had done up to his 42nd year, all his athletic triumphs, barnstorming, and personnel work, merely was preparation for what he now is doing. He is, in common with most of us, a sentimentalist, but he has no sentimental talk about life having been good to him and his duty to pay it back.

It is the individual who counts most in this age, he says, not racial or religious groups or nationalities. To work with and try to help develop the individual is the important thing for Jesse Owens and what remains of his life will be devoted to that.

The Times
Reading Pennsylvania
Tuesday, December 1, 1970

JESSE OWENS SPEAKS TO EDUCATORS
Challenges Teachers to Become More Involved with Their Students

By Terry Mickhart, Staff Writer

In the peppermint-tinged world of sports, Jesse Owens beams through all the hypocrisy and self-gain philosophies like a flood of sunlight on a dreary autumn afternoon.

To the former Olympic champion, sports is not an end, but merely a beginning, a stepping stone. And, for Jesse Owens, the stepping stone provided a bridge between boyhood poverty and the respect of dignified maturity.

Today, the sharecropper's son turned public relations executive works as an independent bridge-builder, constructing stepping stones for others. Employment and education for poor whites and blacks are his goals. And he strives untiringly to achieve them.

"All I'm asking for is the opportunity to do it myself," Owens said Monday afternoon, speaking with the voice which he wishes to hear from those he helps. "And we have to help one another at the same time. As you grow older, you realize that you can't live in this world by yourself."

Owens was in Reading to speak at the Reading School District In-Service Education Program. And, despite several delays in a fog-engulfed airport, he finally arrived to weave his spell-binding web of anecdotes and challenges for the nearly 800 teachers and administrators.

"I guess I'm just not as fast as I used to be," quipped the ex-world record holder in almost every track-and-field event he attempted.

"People always ask me about the 1936 Olympics (when he won four gold medals and established three world records)," he said. "But don't get me wrong—I'm glad they do it. If people forget the Olympics, they forget what Hitler did there and they forget me."

Jesse Owens, however, is not that easy to forget. At 57 years of age, he brims with vitality and good will. He opens himself up to you, but he retains authority. When he speaks, you listen to the ever-fluctuating, yet soothing tones and begin to understand the compassion of the man.

Born James Cleveland Owens in Decatur, Alabama, he moved with his family to Cleveland, Ohio, as a young boy. When he enrolled in grade school, he acquired the name Jesse.

"On the first day of school, my first-grade teacher asked me my name and I said, 'J.C. Owens'," he explained after his speech. "And she said, 'Oh, Jesse,' and I've never considered changing it since."

Proclaimed as the Champion of the Century in 1960, he would be expected to cite the Olympics as his greatest accomplishment. But, for Jesse Owens, life transcends the scope of sports.

"My greatest accomplishment? That would have to be marrying my wife, Ruth," he said with a brightening smile. "We met in junior high school and were married in senior high. Since then, she's been more than just a wife—she's been a confidant and inspiration.

"We have three daughters," he added. "One's a teacher, one's a social worker, and one's a bank executive. The youngest was the Homecoming Queen at Ohio State in 1961. I'm very proud of that, she's the only black girl to be the queen."

The '36 Olympics does qualify as his greatest thrill. "The Olympics is the major leagues of amateur sports," Owens explained. "It's the greatest success one can claim in the field and I consider myself very lucky to have achieved what I did."

Owens does not speak of Hitler's alleged rebuff without probing. And when he does, he dismisses it as a minor incident. To him, Hitler's reference to "America's black cargo" means little. Jesse Owens allows his performance to speak for itself.

"I wouldn't want to change anything in my life and there's nothing else I'd rather be doing now," he indicated. "Sure, I've had ups and downs, but God has been very good to me. If I had a pencil and eraser and could start over again, I couldn't improve anything.

"I feel I'm a lot richer than most people—not in money, but in many aspects of life," he pointed out. "The people I work with and meet in my job and travels (over 150,000 miles a year) are great. They made my work enjoyable.

Yet, even with all those people, Owens singled out one man, his junior-high track coach, Charles Riley, as his most admired. "He had the most influence on my life—everyone loved him and he loved everyone," he said. "He made a lot of things possible for a lot of kids."

Most of today's professional athletes cannot rival the aura Owens possessed in his time, but Jesse still feels that most of them provide good examples for the youth.

"Bart Starr, Gale Sayers, Mike Garrett, Bob Gibson—they all are present symbols with which kids can identify," Owens noted. "Even Cassius Clay is a symbol.

"I know Cassius, but I only know him by his devotion to his lifestyle," he added. "I never argue about religion or politics. After all, Jesus Christ was the most perfect man who ever lived and they nailed him to a cross."

Owens is a graduate of Ohio State University and there was just one inevitable question. "Who's number one (in college football)?" he grinned. "Well, Notre Dame just got beat and I think Texas is going to get belted by Arkansas. So it has to be the Bucks."

The Chicago resident always returns to his stepping-stone philosophy. "Sports have all the ingredients of life," he explained. "First, you're with people. And you're on an even basis with all of them and can figure out the folk way of others. Then you begin to see the good and the bad and the difference in people," he continued. "But, all the time, you don't hate. You work to make things better, instead of being subservient to them."

And, Jesse Owens does work to make things better. He calls it his "civic responsibility," helping with a boys' club and a YMCA in Chicago.

"My main concern is finding employment for people who need it," he said. "Working gives incentive and independence— and that's what these people need. Through my work, I meet many college officials and with their help, I try to get some of these kids into school.

"The athlete can do it by himself—the colleges go after him, but the scholastic ones, they need help," Owens stated. "They have to know the avenues by which they can get into a school."

In his speech, Owens urged . . . no, challenged, the Reading School District teachers to become more involved with their students. "The students are like willow trees and it's up to you to bend them in the right direction," he emphasized.

"They need you to perpetuate leadership, to become involved in more than just classroom problems, to give them the message they need," he boomed over the hallowed silence of the Reading High auditorium.

In sports, Owens maintained that a championship is merely mythical—the trophies tarnish. "But in the game of life, there is the greatest championship of all—and it never becomes tarnished.

"You have to communicate, to find reasons for the lack of incentive and hope, to be totally interested," he said. "You have to take the oath to do this."

Jesse Owens, world-famed athlete and a bridge-builder for the underprivileged, has taken that oath.

The Christian Science Monitor
Tuesday, April 1, 1980

JESSE OWENS: HIS PLACE IN HISTORY

By Larry Eldridge, Sports Editor

Jesse Owens will always be remembered for that one incredible week in Berlin when he made mockery of Adolph Hitler's "master race" theory, but perhaps an even greater legacy is the way he used his fame in later years to help steer thousands of youngsters down the right path.

"This is the big thing in my life now—working with kids and trying to guide them," the hero of the 1936 Olympics told me just last year in his final visit to Boston. "The only thing you can do is say what you feel and hope to have enough charisma that some lives are going to be affected."

Owens, who passed on Monday, certainly had that charisma, as he demonstrated traveling around the country for many years, giving hundreds of speeches annually. The words may have been the standard platitudes about hard work, perseverance, honesty, etc., but Jesse's simple eloquence and obvious sincerity gave them an impact far beyond their literal meanings. He could move any audience, of any age group, to the height of emotion—and of course it didn't hurt his cause with today's hard-to-reach young people that he stood there himself as the personification of the virtues he was preaching.

As a youngster, Owens had it at least as tough as most of those he later counseled. Born Sept. 9, 1913, in Danville, Ala., he spent his earliest years helping his sharecropper father, four brothers, and four sisters pick cotton. When he was nine the family moved to Cleveland, which was an improvement, but it was still no easy lot for a black young-ster growing up during the Depression era of the 1920s and early 1930s.

Young Jesse's rapidly emerging brilliance in track and field propelled him in to the headlines even in junior high school, however, and after a record-breaking collegiate career at Ohio State he climaxed it all with that fabulous Olympic performance—winning both sprints and the broad jump, then earning a fourth gold medal as leadoff man on the victorious Olympic performance—winning both sprints and the broad jump, then earning a fourth gold medal as leadoff man on the victorious U.S. 400-meter relay team. He got no recognition, however, from Hitler, who devel-oped a habit of being absent from his box at times when he might otherwise have been expected to congratulate Jesse for his triumphs.

I first met Owens in 1972—once in Boston where he was promoting one of the many youth track and field meets he ran annually throughout the country, then again in Munich where he was an official guest at the first Olympics held in Germany since those infamous 1936 Games. Naturally I asked him about his recollections.

"Frankly I didn't know too much about what was going on at the time," he told me. "I was concentrating on the guys I was running against, not on people sitting in the stands. You know as much about the incidents as I do. I saw Hitler every day. I didn't come there to shake hands with him.

"The people in the press box always get a much better over-all view of what's going on than the competitors. What they saw is what they wrote about."

Was the part about Hitler snubbing him blown out of proportion, then, as some later historians have suggested?

"No, I don't think it was out of proportion," he said. "I think it probably all happened as reported. It certainly seems consistent with his policies and theories. He left the stadium on occasions when I was competing for what reasons I don't know. Because I was winning, destroying his myth, or whatever."

Owens was famous in track and field circles even before 1936. In 1933 he set a national schoolboy 100-yard dash record of 9.4 seconds which stood for two decades. And in 1935, in one incredible burst at the Big Ten Championships, he set three world records (in the 200 meters, the 200 yard low hurdles, and the broad jump) and tied another (in the 100) in the space of 45 minutes. But it was Berlin that made him a household name—and he was the first to realize that his athletic feats were only part of the reason.

"We were very fortunate from the standpoint of competing," he said to me, "but of course it was the place and the time in history that gave the moment its special significance. Here was a man who affected the lives of the entire world. I was over there competing in his own backyard. He was on the rise, preaching his doctrines, and we just happened to make his doctrines not come true—because I'm sure not blond and blue-eyed!"

After the Olympics Owens tried to exploit his fame, but those times were a far cry from today with its million-dollar TV and advertising opportunities for Olympic heroes, and many of his early ventures failed to pan out.

"That was a time when the blacks of America had a tough time economically and recognition-wise," he explained. "The opportunities just weren't there. America was just beginning to awaken to the realization that God made us all, and if a man has ability the color of his skin doesn't matter. It took a long while to learn this, and of course we still have pockets of resistance, but we've come a long way since the 1930s and 1940s."

Eventually Owens found his niche, though, building his own public relations firm into a successful business and directing most of his other available time into community service, especially youth work. His pet project over the last several years was an annual competition called the Jesse Owens Games, consisting of track and field meets for boys and girls between the ages of nine and 15, starting on a regional basis and culminating in a national championship. He felt very strongly about the positive effects of such competitions in bringing people together—from youth meets like this all the way up to the Olympics. "When you see thousands of young people together—eating, dancing, singing, practicing together, then competing against each other," he said of the Olympic atmosphere, "you know it just has to eventually bring a new kind of understanding of other people and other nations' folkways. This is a wonderful thing, because these young people are the greatest commodity the world has."

Despite this feeling, Owens issued a statement earlier this year supporting President Carter in his decision that the United States should not go to Moscow this summer.

"As a member and backer of the Olympic Committee and advocate of the Olympic movement, I am first, last, and always an American," Owens said. "If the president feels that for political reasons we should not go, I'll back the president 100 percent. I regret that it has to be that way, and hope the political situation will cool down."

My own fondest memory of Jesse is from that appearance in Boston a few months earlier. Since speaking with him in 1972 I had had occasion to talk with his Olympic teammate Mack Robinson, who had finished second by four-tenths of a second in the 200 meter race. Robinson reminisced about how his shoes were not right, how he was supposed to have gotten a new pair, and how he was sure the result would have been different if only someone hadn't made a mistake and failed to get them to him. So just to see what Jesse would say, I mentioned this to him.

The winner of all that Olympic gold could easily have pooh-poohed the whole thing, as indeed a lot of athletes would have. But Jesse wasn't about to take himself that seriously.

"Well, I'm glad he didn't get those shoes then," he said with a smile.

By Larry Eldridge. Reproduced with permission from the April 1, 1980 issue of The Christian Science Monitor (www.csmonitor.com <http://www.csmonitor.com/>).

Appendix B:
Distribution of the
Olympic Medals at the
1936 Summer Olympics

Distribution of the Olympic Medals
at the 1936 Summer Olympics
(by country)

This is the full table of the medal count of the 1936 Summer Olympics. These rankings sort by the number of gold medals earned by a country. The number of silvers is taken into consideration next and then the number of bronze. If, after the above, countries are still tied, equal ranking is given and they are listed alphabetically.

RANK	COUNTRY	GOLD	SILVER	BRONZE	TOTAL
1	Germany	33	26	30	89
2	United States	24	20	12	56
3	Hungary	10	1	5	16
4	Italy	8	9	5	22
5	Finland	7	6	6	19
6	France	7	6	6	19
7	Sweden	6	5	9	20
8	Netherlands	6	4	7	17
9	Japan	5	4	7	16
10	Great Britain	4	7	3	14
11	Austria	4	6	3	13
12	Czechoslovakia	3	5	0	8
13	Argentina	2	2	3	7

Rank	Country	Gold	Silver	Bronze	Total
14	Estonia	2	2	3	7
15	Egypt	2	1	2	5
16	Switzerland	1	9	5	15
17	Canada	1	3	5	9
18	Norway	1	3	1	5
19	Korea	1	0	1	2
20	Turkey	1	0	0	1
21	New Zealand	1	0	0	1
22	India	1	0	0	1
23	Poland	0	3	3	6
24	Denmark	0	2	3	5
25	Latvia	0	1	1	2
26	Romania	0	1	0	1
27	South Africa	0	1	0	1
28	Yugoslavia	0	1	0	1
29	Mexico	0	0	3	3
30	Belgium	0	0	2	2
31	Australia	0	0	1	1
32	Portugal	0	0	1	1
33	Philippines	0	0	1	1

1913   Born James Cleveland Owens on September 12 in Oakville, Alabama

ca. 1922   Moves to Cleveland, Ohio

1927   Enrolls at Fairmount Junior High School; meets Coach Charles Riley

1930   Enrolls at East Technical High School

1933   Equals the world record in the 100-yard dash and breaks the world record in the 220-yard dash at the National Interscholastic Meet; enrolls at Ohio State University

1935   Breaks five world records and ties a sixth at the Big Ten Championships; marries Minnie Ruth Solomon

1936   Breaks the world record in the 100-yard dash; earns a berth on the U.S. Olympic team; wins Olympic gold medals in the 100 meters, 200 meters, long jump, and 400-meter relay; signs agency contract; loses amateur status

1937   Becomes a bandleader and the owner of a basketball team, softball team, and dry-cleaning company

1940   Resumes studies at Ohio State University

1941   Placed in charge of the Civilian Defense Office's national physical fitness program; takes a personnel job with Ford Motor Company

1945   Launches a public relations company

1950   Named the greatest track-and-field athlete in history by the Associated Press; appointed head of Illinois's Athletic Commission and Youth Commission; begins to travel widely as goodwill ambassador for the State Department

1965   Serves as running coach for the New York Mets

1970 Publishes *Blackthink: My Life as Black Man and White Man* and *The Jesse Owens Story*; awarded an honorary doctor of athletic arts degree from Ohio State University

1972 Publishes *I Have Changed*

1980 Dies of lung cancer on March 31 in Tucson, Arizona

Ashe, Arthur. *A Hard Road to Glory*. New York: Amistad-Warner, 1988.

Baker, William J. *Jesse Owens: An American Life*. New York: Free Press, 1986.

Cromwell, Dean B. *Championship Technique in Track and Field: A Book for Athletes, Coaches, and Spectators*. New York: McGraw-Hill, 1941.

Edwards, Harry. *The Revolt of the Black Athlete*. New York: Free Press, 1969.

Hart-Davis, Duff. *Hitler's Games*. New York: Harper & Row, 1986.

Johnson, William O., Jr. *All That Glitters Is Not Gold: The Olympic Games*. New York: Putnam, 1972.

Kusmer, Kenneth L. *A Ghetto Takes Shape: Black Cleveland*. Urbana: University of Illinois Press, 1976.

Mandell, Richard D. *The Nazi Olympics*. New York: Macmillan, 1971.

Owens, Jesse. *Blackthink: My Life as Black Man and White Man*. New York: William Morrow, 1970.

———. *I Have Changed*. New York: Morrow, 1972.

———. *Jesse: A Spiritual Autobiography*. Plainfield, NJ: Logos International, 1978.

———. *The Jesse Owens Story*. New York: Putnam, 1970.

Robertson, Lawson. *Modern Athletics*. New York: Scribners, 1932.

Wallechinsky, David. *The Complete Book of the Olympics*. New York: Viking Press, 1984.

WEBSITES

Athens 2004.
www.cbc.ca/olympics/history/1936.html

Jesse Owens. The Official Web Site.
www.jesseowens.com

The Jesse Owens Foundation.
www.jesse-owens.org

Official Website of the Olympic Movement.
www.olympic.org

World Olympians Association.
www.woaolympians.com

ESPN biography.
www.espn.go.com/classic/biography/s/Owens_Jesse.html

page:

3:	Associated Press, AP	44:	Associated Press, AP
6:	Associated Press, AP	51:	© Bettmann/CORBIS
12:	The Cleveland Public Library	55:	Associated Press, AP
14:	The Cleveland Public Library	60:	Special Collections, The
20:	Associated Press, AP		New York Public Library,
23:	© Bettmann/CORBIS		Astor, Lennox, and Tilden
26:	Ohio State University Archives		Foundation
28:	Ohio State University Archives	63:	Ohio State University Archives
30:	© Bettmann/CORBIS	68:	© Bettmann/CORBIS
40:	© Hulton|Archive by	77:	Associated Press, AP
	Getty Images, Inc.		

Cover: © Getty Images

ABOUT THE AUTHOR

Tony Gentry holds an honors degree in history and literature from Harvard College. Formerly an award-winning news and feature editor at WWL Newsradio in New Orleans, he now works in New York City, where he is an avid runner. His poetry and short stories have been published in *Turnstile* and *Downtown*. He is also the author of *Paul Laurence Dunbar* in the BLACK AMERICANS OF ACHIEVEMENT series.

CONSULTING EDITOR, REVISED EDITION

Heather Lehr Wagner is a writer and editor. She is the author of 30 books exploring social and political issues and focusing on the lives of prominent Americans and has contributed to biographies of *Alex Haley*, *Langston Hughes*, and *Colin Powell* in the BLACK AMERICANS OF ACHIEVEMENT Legacy Editions. She earned a BA in political science from Duke University and an MA in government from the College of William and Mary. She lives with her husband and family in Pennsylvania.

CONSULTING EDITOR, FIRST EDITION

Nathan Irvin Huggins was W.E.B. Du Bois Professor of History and Director of the W.E.B. Du Bois Institute for Afro-American Research at Harvard University. He previously taught at Columbia University. Professor Huggins was the author of numerous books, including *Black Odyssey: The Afro-American Ordeal in Slavery*, *The Harlem Renaissance*, and *Slave and Citizen: The Life of Frederick Douglass*. Nathan I. Huggins died in 1989.